WILMATH

WILMATH

By

KAY BRAND

Kelley,
I hope you
enjoy reading my
book!
Kay (Brand) Gott

Leathers Publishing
A division of Squire Publishers, Inc.
4500 College Blvd.
Leawood, KS 66211
1/888/888-7696

Printed in the United States

ISBN: 1-58597-041-7

Library of Congress Number: 00134027

LEATHERS PUBLISHING

A division of Squire Publishers, Inc.
4500 College Blvd.
Leawood, KS 66211
1/888/888-7696

ACKNOWLEDGMENTS

The author wishes to express her appreciation and gratitude to Eva McCarty of Hurdland, Missouri, for her help in sharing records, photos and information which made this work possible.

Ernest H. Dent, Kirksville, Missouri, also supplied the author with information. He was of great help in sharing his personal recollections and experiences relating to this book.

Heartfelt thanks go to Maise Dennis, of Dallas, Texas, for providing invaluable information and photos. She's one terrific lady who is devoted to her family.

FOREWORD

"Wilmath" is a tale based on the life of Wilmath Dennis Garren, as the author has seen it. Some of the events, circumstances and almost all of the conversations that take place in the book are fictional. The writer has invented some characters that never existed and added non-existing events and circumstances to enhance the reader's enjoyment and make the story more realistic.

The author's purpose in writing the book is to share a story that she hopes will captivate the reader as much as it did her. It is an unusual story of a woman who met many obstacles and challenges throughout her life with strength and courage and, in the process, gained the respect she longed for.

DEDICATION

This book is respectfully dedicated
to
Eva McCarty

CHAPTER ONE

August 8, 1894

A WARM BREEZE tugged at the old tattered lace curtain, flapping it gently against the open bedroom window. The sun had begun to rise, casting a narrow band of light across the old straw mattress that lay on a crude wooden bed frame. Wilmath was already awake; in fact, she'd slept very little throughout the night. Her thoughts immediately became immersed in the happenings of the day ahead — this was her wedding day!

She rose from the bed and made her way to the old chest of drawers and gazed sleepily into the oval mirror hanging on the wall above the chest. As she lit the wick of the old kerosene lamp that was sitting on a nearby table, the flame flickered uncertainly at first, reminding her that she was filled with much of that same feeling herself.

The image peering back at her in the mirror looked very mature for a girl of 13. Dark brown hair framed a youthful cherubic face. Her eyelids drooped slightly downward over her blue eyes, giving them an almost brooding look.

Wilmath could hear the clattering of utensils coming from the kitchen downstairs. Her mother, Paulina Dennis, was most likely baking bread for the day on the old wood cook stove. She knew Ma was hustling about, trying to finish with the morning tasks that required the use of the hot oven. August days in southeastern Adair County, Missouri, could be scorchers, and this one already was proving to be no exception.

This will be the last day I'll eat a meal in this house for awhile, she thought sadly. Her mind began wandering — thinking back to all the meals Ma had cooked in the house — all the cleaning and laundry she'd done — it was overwhelming!

Paulina Moore had married Simon Peter Dennis in 1883, when Wilmath was two. "Pete" was 25 years older than Paulina when they married and settled on the farm two miles northeast of La Plata. He'd bought the property in the fall of '82, just a few short months after a bitter and lengthy divorce from his first wife, Martha J. Reid Dennis. Martha came from a well-to-do family near Cherry Box, in Shelby County. Soon after the divorce, the children had started traveling back and forth between Cherry Box and their father's farm near La Plata. Martha and Pete were the parents of eight children, six of them still living. Charles, Phoebe Roselle (Rosie) and John were all grown and living on their own. Daniel, Seba, and Lorenzo (Ren) lived with their mother, who had married a man named William Penrod two years after her divorce from Pete.

Paulina and Pete had five children (commonly referred to as the "second Dennis family"). They were Vivian, Victor, Earl, Orena and Amy. Wilmath thought about the fact that Ma was always swamped with kids and would always be tied down. She'd never have a house full of kids and live like that, she silently promised herself.

Her thoughts began to center on the day's upcoming event once more, as she was donning her homemade undergarments. This was to be her wedding day — the day every girl dreamed of. Wilmath had envisioned a much different kind of day for herself. For one thing, she was only 13 years old! She was not certain why Ma and Pete were forcing her to marry Pete's son, John Dennis. The main reason they'd given concerned the fact that some of the stepbrothers had made footprints on the ground directly below her bedroom window. They had told their folks a trumped-up story about John climbing up to her room at night.

"That story is simply not true, Ma," she had staunchly denied with tears in her eyes. Nevertheless, Ma seemed to believe the brothers' story — maybe even thinking she was "in the family way"— as folks around there always put it. Well, she wasn't, and she'd told Ma over and over that she didn't see why they were insisting that she marry that "old" man! John Dennis was 26 years old and had been married before. He'd had no children of that marriage, but his former wife, Alice Davis Dennis, had two little boys. The marriage had only lasted three years.

Wilmath looked now at the clothing she'd so carefully laid

out the night before — it wasn't nearly as nice as the wedding attire that Sarah Wilson, who lived three miles up the road toward Wilson Town, had worn at her fancy wedding. I'll do the very best I can, considering the circumstances, she consoled herself. She got out the metal curling iron from the top drawer of the chest and held it over the lamp's flame, getting it hot enough to place a few curls around her forehead. She grasped two tiny wisps of hair hanging in front of each ear and made a small dangling curl that spiraled down each side of her cheeks. She pulled her long dark hair back tightly from her face, securing it with a ribbon at the base of her neck. Peering into the mirror once more, she decided that fixing her hair in this fashion had given her face a much softer image.

She slipped on the white long-sleeved blouse that she had borrowed from her stepsister, Rosie Thorn, who lived in Edina. Then she put on the long brown skirt that Ma had made over for her that had belonged to Paulina's sister, Ellen. The only new thing she had was the wide black belt with pearl buttons that her mother had bought at the dry goods store in La Plata. After lacing up her black boots, she stared approvingly at herself in the mirror. Wilmath stood tall and straight, her shoulders back, her mature breasts jutting out significantly over her tiny waist, which was made even smaller by the laced-up corset she wore beneath her outer garments.

Ma was calling from downstairs; Wilmath walked down the narrow staircase slowly, her eyes devouring all the familiar furnishings coming into view as she reached the bottom of the stairs. It was the only home she'd ever known! Hanging on the wall, which was papered in faded cabbage roses, near the entrance to the sitting room was a huge oval picture of Paulina, Pete and all the children, including Wilmath. She paused a moment and noticed how much she resembled her mother. Paulina was a large woman, getting heavier as she got older. Her dark hair was always parted in the middle and her hair pulled straight back and coiled in a bun at the back of her round neck. Pete's white hair, mustache and flowing full beard reflected the age difference of 25 years between him and his wife. A tall, thin man, his most outstanding feature was his eyes, which were blue in color and quite piercing at times.

Wilmath liked Pete — he'd been the only father she'd ever

known. She had no idea about the identity of her real father. Paulina had told her that his name wasn't important, as she hadn't seen him since the evening he had walked out of her life forever. She further explained that when she was 22, she had gone to stay with her married sister, Ellen, who lived 18 miles northeast of Kirksville in a town called Wilmathsville. The general store there was owned by a kind, older lady, Mrs. Wilmath McLean, for whom the town was named. Mrs. McLean's daughter, Belle, ran the only boarding house in town, and it was here that a young drummer, who peddled his wares at the general store, stayed when he came to the area. He had become romantically involved with Paulina; she fondly looked forward to his visits. One day Belle had come to Ellen's house and asked to see Paulina, with a package in her hands. Belle had received a note with it, which she had with her. The young man had written a few short lines to Belle, explaining that he would not be coming to Wilmathsville again and asked her to deliver the small parcel to Paulina.

Paulina opened the package, and, there, in the box, lined with black felt, was a strand of pearls. Although she thought they were beautiful, the broken-hearted girl couldn't bear the thought of wearing them and put them in the bottom of her trunk. Several months later she discovered that she was "with child." Her little daughter was born June 15, 1881, at Ellen's house, with old Mrs. McLean and Belle at her side. Paulina decided to name her baby girl Wilmath, due to the friendship that had been extended to her by the McLeans.

Presently, Wilmath became aware of the amount of heat already engulfing the downstairs. The old oven had warmed up the house considerably, and the temperature outside was escalating as well.

"Good morning, daughter," Paulina uttered cheerfully. "Did you sleep well?"

"No, Ma, I didn't — I thought about this marriage all night and I don't want to do this — it's a mistake!"

"Now, listen, girl — John's older and will be what you need in a husband. You're a big girl for your age — you'll be fine!"

"But, Ma, he's too old for me and I don't love him, and, besides, he's my stepbrother."

"Well, it could be worse — no one might want to marry you."

"Of course, they would — when it's time — I'm just too young to get married now!"

"Nonsense — why Pete's already taken the team and wagon over to Cherry Box to fetch John. They'll be here before long."

Wilmath bit her lip and tried to hold back the tears. How could Ma insist on something that would be so wrong for her! Her thoughts wandered, as she looked out the east kitchen window, out beyond the old weather-beaten porch, to where the leafed-out trees and timber hid the railroad tracks from view in the summer. She heard the whistle of the Santa Fe engine; then she finally saw snatches of train cars as it chugged along the tracks that ran north up toward Gibbs.

In 1888, the Santa Fe Railroad built a track that sliced through the Dennis property, going northward to Gibbs. Wilson Town was a thriving trading center at the time, but the railroad wanted the most direct route possible from Kansas City to Chicago. The grading on the railroad was done with the labor of horses and mules. These animals were boarded at the Dennis farm at night, as well as at other farms along the route. Local men were hired to work on the project, and Gibbs was literally "put on the map" by the railroad. Just last February, the town had been incorporated as a village. She remembered all the hours she and her sisters and brothers had spent counting railroad cars, even playing along the tracks when Ma wasn't around.

Her thoughts of the past continued, as she thought of the wooded area between the barn lot and the tracks. It was the location of her "special spot," near the "crick." The crick was really Titus Creek, a branch of the Chariton River. It was so shallow that it ran dry during the summer months of July and August.

Her "spot" became special when she had gone there one day when she was 11, to be alone. Ma had sent her to the woods to pick persimmons in the fall. Vic and Earl had been sent along to shimmy up the tree and knock the ripe fruit to the ground so that they might fill the pail Wilmath carried and take them to Ma to make jelly. After the boys had shaken off all the fruit that would budge, Wilmath had picked them up off the ground, and the pail was full. The two boys grabbed the pail and started throwing persimmons everywhere! Wilmath, not to be outdone, held her own with her young brothers, who were big for their age. Soon, all the fruit was being scattered here and yon, the bucket almost empty. They heard the grass snapping behind them, and there stood Ma, hands on her hips, surveying the damage.

"Whose idea was this?" she bellowed at them.

Vic spoke first. "Why, Ma, Willie's older than us, and she started it all."

"No, Ma, that's not right — these boys are lyin'. We had a nice pail full of fruit almost ready to bring to the house, then Vic and Earl started throwin' them."

"She started it, Ma," chimed in Earl. Wilmath knew there was no use arguing with Ma — she always believed those boys.

"Well, little miss, maybe we better take you to the smokehouse and get this straightened out," Ma commanded authoritatively. She grabbed the girl by the hand and led her to the outbuilding up by the house, giving her what she deemed "a good licking."

Half an hour later, Seba Dennis had stopped at the farm to see his father. Wilmath had run down to sit by the creek to be by herself. She saw Seba making his way down to the woods, and he finally came and sat down beside the sad girl. Her stepbrother was only three years older than Wilmath and lived at Cherry Box with his mother, Martha. He was so special — not at all like the rest of the boys — he was taller and was built bigger overall. His treatment of Wilmath had always been kind.

"Wilmath, what're you doin' down here all by yourself?" he asked.

"Oh, Seba," she sobbed, and began telling him how her younger brothers had managed to get her in trouble with the persimmons.

He sat down and held her hand. "I know it's hard livin' with those two young ruffians and you bein' the oldest and a half-sister, at that. Listen, you're getting closer to bein' a young woman now — before you know it, you'll be grown and have a family of your own. Paulina means well, I'm sure. It's just that she's got a lot of work with those kids, and you're the oldest. She depends on you so much. Vivian and Orena aren't old enough to do most of the chores yet. There'll be a better day — you'll see." Wilmath, comforted by his words, felt much better — Seba had a way about him.

From that day on, as long as she could remember, when Seba came by, they'd go to her special place. One day, he was swinging on some grapevines that grew wild along the creek bank.

"Come and join me," he insisted. They had such fun! He was carefree and spirited, and so was she. Wilmath decided that she and Seba had much in common, besides their family relationship. After they'd grown tired of riding back and forth across the creek, they lay down in the grass to rest and talk. She liked that — she hung on his every word — listening intently. He was going to be much more polished than the other Dennis boys, she decided.

He had noticed that she was twirling something green around in her hands.

"What have you got there?" he asked curiously. She opened her hand up fully now, revealing a four-leafed clover that lay in her palm.

"I think this means that this is my lucky day," she confided to him.

Seba reached in his pocket and displayed a worn pocketknife and said, "Let's carve our initials in the trunk of this old elm tree."

Wilmath shuddered with delight, her blue eyes sparkling. "Yes, let's do — who knows — maybe some day we'll get married and travel to some of the faraway places we've only read about and dreamed of!"

Seba chuckled, "Well, we've got a few years before we even think of that, don't we?" Soon, there in the trunk of the elm, etched deep into the bark, was the shape of two entwined hearts with the initials " S.D." on one, and "W. M." on the other. Uttering no words, Seba turned, put his long arms around her, pulled her to him and kissed her lightly on the lips. Then, hand in hand, the two "friends" walked up to the house. Wilmath knew she'd never forget that moment — it would be embedded in her heart forever!

Now, her thoughts being interrupted by the sight of Paulina going from the kitchen to the bedroom, she silently cried within herself — Why, oh, why, can't I be marrying Seba today instead of his older brother? She would ask herself that question many times in the days ahead.

Paulina was now in the tiny bedroom just across from the sitting room, rummaging around in the old trunk that had sat in the south corner of the room ever since Wilmath could remember. After delving to the bottom of the trunk and uprooting the items stored on top, Paulina produced a small box and brought it into the kitchen, beckoning her daughter to follow.

"Here, I want you to have this now — it's fittin'." Paulina had a lump in her throat as she handed Wilmath the box. Wilmath knew what would be in there, even before she looked. Nestled in the old black felt lining of the box was the pearl necklace. Wilmath put it on and reached up and kissed her mother on the cheek.

"Thanks, Ma — I'll take good care of it always."

After having only a slice of Ma's bread and some butter, Wilmath looked out the front door just in time to see Pete and John driving up the lane — Pete was holding the reins, and John was by his side. This was the man she was expected to marry today. John was a stern man, who smiled little. He sat up straight and proper beside his dad, but little else about him was proper, Wilmath noticed.

John was fairly tall, slender, with light brown hair and a brown mustache. The corners of his mouth turned up in a sullen manner. His brown suit was well worn, and his white shirt was wrinkled and gray. He had made a halfway attempt to shine his old boots, which were also well worn.

Paulina had rushed into the bedroom to change into her one good dress for the occasion. John and Pete entered the house, and John came up to Wilmath with his arms extended.

"Well, little girl, are you ready to tie the knot?" he asked. Wilmath nodded in silent surrender. Old Pete needed a clean shirt, and it was nearly noon when the wedding party headed out the door. Paulina paused to pick up a basket of food that was sitting just inside the kitchen. She had fresh vegetables, canned pork and two loaves of bread tucked inside. Pete went out through the back porch and walked outside toward the old pump that stood over the well. He drew some cool drinking water in a large bucket to take along to drink as they rode to La Plata in the wagon. Reaching for the metal cup that was hanging near the pump, he hurried to place the bucket and cup in the wagon next to the food and climbed up to the front, taking the reins in hand. The women, who were sitting in the back, felt the heat radiating from the wagon seats, even through all the clothing they wore. Paulina got out the food, and John and Pete took turns driving the wagon while they ate. Wilmath ate little — her stomach was queasy, and she wasn't about to make matters worse by eating.

The Dennis' drove past their closest neighbor's house as they headed down the dusty dirt road. Mrs. Samantha Jenkins was hanging out clothes on the clothesline.

She waved to them and called out, "Good luck to you young folks!"

There had been little rain in Adair County since July. The corn, growing tall in the fields, had begun to get brown edges on its green stalks. Pete and John talked of crops and livestock, while Wilmath sat quietly with Paulina. They had to hurry to get to La Plata. The Wabash would be stopping there for passengers at 1 p.m. Pete slapped harder on the reins, and the wagon went faster down the dirt roads to town.

The town of La Plata was located in Macon County. It was just north of town that the Adair County line began. The Dennis' did most of their trading in La Plata, as it was the town closest to their farm.

Pete got out of the wagon first and walked over to the depot ticket window.

"Four tickets to Kirksville," he shouted at the nearly deaf old Mr. Stone, the ticket master. John had gone to the Goodson Livery Stable to leave the team and wagon, and the two ladies sat on a straight wooden bench outside the depot. About 20 minutes later, they heard the roar of the train's engine, and, in a few moments it pulled into sight. It slowed to a stop, and several people disembarked from the train's passenger car. The wedding party boarded the train for their destination, Kirksville, which was 17 miles away. The engine puffed along slowly at first, gathering speed as it passed along the countryside. When they reached Millard, the only stop between La Plata and Kirksville, they saw a man with a pouch of mail waiting outside the small stop. The train slowed long enough for the man to hand the mail to a conductor who stayed on board. Onward to Kirksville they traveled.

Thirty minutes later, the train was pulling to a stop beside the small wooden structure currently serving as the depot at Kirksville. One block farther down the tracks, a larger, more modern building, currently under construction, would replace the older depot. The Dennis' stepped off the train onto the board sidewalk and headed toward the town's square.

Kirksville was the county seat of Adair County. The courthouse, which was erected in 1853, had burned in 1865. The county hadn't had a courthouse in 30 years. The square had become a sort of park filled with trees. Some residents of the county had wanted to build a new courthouse at a different location, leaving the square for a public park. Others wanted the square reserved for a courthouse. The debate was still going on, and the county was using several rooms upstairs over a building across the street from the square as the present courthouse.

Pete, Paulina, John and Wilmath entered the building, heading upstairs to the office where marriage licenses were issued. Pete and Paulina had to give their permission for their daughter to marry, because of her young age. Wilmath had hardly spoken since they'd left home. The heat had straightened and wilted the curls on each side of her face. Her undergarments were damp with perspiration.

I will soon be a changed woman, she thought. I'll be somebody's wife! She could hardly fathom the idea! Pete soon came out of the license office, followed by his wife.

"Wilmath, dear, the justice of the peace is waiting in the room next door to perform your marriage now," Pete said softly. She smoothed her hair as neatly as possible, stood up straight, and marched into the room behind her parents. John followed.

"I don't have a ring for you yet," he whispered apologetically. "I'll get you one later after I cut some wood this winter."

"It's okay with me," she whispered back. She really didn't care, as nothing else about this day was like she would have planned it. Old B. W. Ross, who was mayor of Kirksville as well as a justice of the peace, sat with his gray head bent down at his desk — his glasses resting comfortably on his long beak-like nose. He looked up as the party entered.

"Good day," he greeted them. "I'm Mayor Ross, and I understand you folks are ready to be married and everything is in order." He was looking at the paper that John had just handed him.

"Yes, sir, I believe so," replied John, exuding confidence. He reached for Wilmath's hand and drew her close beside him. The mayor began reading to them from a book and then from the Bible, but Wilmath heard little of it. Her mind was still rebelling against the idea, but she knew she was already trapped! John recited the vows after the old man, and then Wilmath said hers. In a few minutes, she heard the words "man and wife" being proclaimed, and it was all over!

They left the courthouse and walked to the depot the same way they'd come about an hour ago. This time John insisted that Wilmath walk along beside him, and she obliged. As they were walking along the old board sidewalk, John noticed that his new bride was taking care to step over the cracks in the walk.

"What're you doin' that for?" he asked.

"Don't want to bring on any more bad luck," she muttered, without looking up.

"Aw, come on — that's just some silly old story," he chided her. Nevertheless, Wilmath continued straddling the cracks all the way to the train depot.

Pete bought the tickets to La Plata. It was late afternoon — he'd get back to the farm just in time to do the evening chores before dark. When the train stopped at La Plata, Pete and Paulina departed — Paulina giving her daughter and new son-in-law each a big hug. John purchased two tickets to Love Lake, where he had a house waiting for them. They sat at the depot on the bench, waiting for the train, receiving little relief from the heat, even though the sun had started to set. Finally, the train arrived.

As they sat on the train, John took Wilmath's hand in his, "You'll be fine," he assured her. "Just wait until you see the lake and have a home to care for." Wilmath decided that maybe she would like the place and the idea of having a house she could call her own.

She squeezed John's hand and said, "I can't wait to see the lake — I've heard how lovely it is."

By the time they reached the general store that stood along the Wabash tracks at Love Lake, Wilmath, exhausted from the heat and stress of the day, had fallen asleep. John nudged her gently. It was almost dark, and as they got off the train he told her they'd have to walk three miles to their place, as he didn't own a team and wagon yet. His brother, Charles, who lived down the road from them, had worked in the fields late and couldn't come to pick them up at the store where the train had left them.

"You're a young girl — you've got two good feet — let's get going." Wilmath was glad she'd had a rest on the train — from what she understood now, she would have to wait until morning to see the lake and assess her new surroundings. They walked until after dark and finally reached a small two-room house.

"Here we are, my little bride," he said. "Let's go in and start our new life." He pushed the rickety door open, and Wilmath entered her new home at Love Lake, and the first part of her new life as Mrs. John Dennis!

CHAPTER TWO

WHEN WILMATH WOKE UP, she couldn't remember where she was. Oh, yes, this was her new home — Love Lake, and her wedding had taken place yesterday. She thought about last night — they'd gotten to this place on foot in the dark. John had lit an old lamp that was sitting on the crude kitchen table. She had noticed then that the furniture in their new home was sparse. There were only two rooms — the kitchen and an adjoining room that served as a sitting room and bedroom. Wilmath decided that she would have to change some things to make the house seem like a home. John suggested that they retire early, as the day had been long and tiring. She felt as weak and shaky as a new colt — she didn't know what to expect as a wife! Ma had said she'd be okay, so she'd do the best that she could. John sat down on the straw mattress. It was covered with an old dingy cloth, with only an old patchwork quilt that was well worn on top of it.

"Come on, Willie, I'll treat you right," he said softly, unbuttoning his shirt. Reluctantly, she joined her new husband on the bed. The "ordeal," as she thought of it, was not much and had very little romance attached to it. She soon heard him snoring and she thought — Now I can lay here and relax!

John had not been in the house when Wilmath woke, but presently she could hear him coming in the door. She quickly dressed, leaving the thoughts of the previous night behind.

"Well, my little girl — are you ready to explore your new surroundings?" he asked.

"How about breakfast?"

"I've been up quite some time, and I've already eaten with Charley and Mira earlier this morning."

"Ma sent us a loaf of bread," she offered, as she reached into a small basket that Paulina had thoughtfully fixed for her.

"You eat that, and then we'll go exploring."

Soon they were walking in a wooded area. The house that they occupied was situated in a small clearing among the timber. John was busy showing her around her new home.

"I'm buyin' this place from my ma — it's been in the Reid family for years. Charley, he's buyin' his farm that way, too. Grandma Reid owns some acreage around here. Ren's gonna move up here soon 'cause he's marryin' Mollie Davidson. Ma's gonna have to sign for him, and Mollie's folks'll have to sign for her since they're so young! Seba was plannin' on movin' here in the cabin next to Charley's, but when he found out Ren was getting married, he decided to help them out by lettin' them move there instead."

We really didn't leave home, thought Wilmath! All the stepbrothers lived down here close together! How she wished Seba was living here, too!

They crossed the same bridge they'd crossed the night before in the dark. John told her that Long Branch got out over here at Mitchell Birch's place when it rained a lot and sometimes made it impossible for folks to get home until the water receded. As they made their way to the general store, John suggested that they buy some staples and supplies and leave them there while they went down to the lake to swim and cool off for a spell. Wilmath thought that seemed like a good idea. They told Ora Ketchum, who ran the store, that they'd be back for their purchases, and then they headed toward Love Lake.

The lake was owned by the Wabash Railroad, which used it as a source of water for their steam engines. This body of water sprawled along the east side of the tracks and encompassed about 20 acres of land. Rowboats were lined up along its eastern shore. Most of the land east of the lake was owned by John Ketchum, a wealthy stockman. He also owned the general store. John Ketchum's property, known as Lakeview Farm, covered 620 acres and was indeed a showplace! He specialized in raising Chester white hogs, as well as raising livestock. He had served on the school board and had been very active in community and political affairs.

"That there's the richest man in Love Lake," John pointed out, as they passed the Ketchums'.

There were two bathhouses farther down on the lake — one

for men and one for women. Wilmath went in one, while John entered the other. In a matter of minutes she appeared in a dark one-piece flannel suit that covered most of her body. He had simply put on a pair of old threadbare trousers and had taken off his shirt. The temperature was almost 95 degrees. When they jumped into the water, they found that the sun had warmed it well for them!

Wilmath had fun — laughing and splashing, while John swam profusely, heading for the opposite shore. He got out of the water and yelled, "Come on, Willie," loud enough to create an echo all over the lake. She swam over to him. After sitting under a shady ash tree for awhile, they decided it was time to go back to the other shore. There they changed their clothes and went to retrieve the goods they'd left at the general store earlier. Walking around to the back of the store with their purchases in their arms, John sat the groceries down on the ground, got out a knife and cut a chunk off a brick of cheese. Then Wilmath produced some crackers, and they stood under a tree eating enough to tide them over until supper. Spying an old well close by, they pumped water to drink, using the tin cup that was attached to the pump by some old rusty wire. Soon they started for home — the sun was slowly sinking in the west.

"Tomorrow, I'm puttin' up hay at the McGinnis place, so pack me a lunch, girl," John informed her. Good, she thought — I'll have the day to myself to plan and figure out how to make my new home more livable!

After John left the next day, Wilmath made a list of things she would need from the store — material, thread — she'd sew up some curtains. She'd forgotten to get vinegar to wash windows with at the store yesterday. She'd get this house whipped into shape the best she knew how! Then she'd walk down the road to Charley's to see Almira and their family.

"Oh, Wilmath, I'm so glad you came to see us," said Almira Dennis, receptively. Wilmath could see the four-year-old twins, John and James, and two-year-old Sam standing behind her at the door. She decided that she was going to enjoy being around her new sister-in-law, who insisted immediately that she call her "Mira." Mira Dennis was a slender young woman of medium height and had pleasant blue eyes. After talking with her for an hour or so, Wilmath decided that one of Mira's greatest attributes was the common sense she seemed to possess.

"When will Ren and Mollie be moving up here?" she asked her new sister-in-law.

"I understand it will be in just a few weeks," Mira informed her.

After worrying about overstaying her welcome, Wilmath rose to leave. Mira hugged her and told her to come by again soon. Wilmath reciprocated by inviting Mira to her house as well.

For several weeks, Wilmath worked continuously, trying to get the house in order. John put up hay at first one place and then another. He had been working over at Sila Doggett's the last day or so. Hay hands were in big demand — it was the second cutting right now. John told her that they had little money to spend on things other than necessary items. It was lucky that Paulina had taught Wilmath at a young age how to "make do" with what was available!

In the fall, John had started shucking corn for various neighbors. Wilmath spent early evenings writing letters up home to Ma and the family in La Plata. Cooking and cleaning kept her busy, and she was enjoying the friendship of her sister-in-law, Mira, and one of the neighbor ladies, Emma Corman. The Cormans lived on down the road from the Dennis' — about two miles south of Charley's. Emma and her husband, John, had been married four years. John was 59 years old, while Emma was 37. They lived in a two-story farmhouse and could afford to live comfortably. The couple had adopted two boys — Matthew was ten, and James B. was eight. The boys' parents had been killed in a train wreck down at Moberly. John thought the boys would be good help on the farm in a few years. Emma confided in Wilmath and told her that she could never have any children of her own. She had married John Corman in Shelby County, the principal reason being that she was already past 30, and it seemed to Emma that life might be passing her by! She could have ended up being an old maid! She was not very tall and had dark brown hair. Her worst feature was a long nose, which seemed to swoop forward and extend down toward her lips, almost covering the top part of her upper lip. Unknown to her, folks in the area referred to her as "Mrs. Big Nose Corman." However, Wilmath only thought of Emma as a good woman and kind friend.

Winter came to Love Lake. John hadn't worked for a spell.

There was even less money for food and clothing. The only clothes Wilmath had were those she had brought with her from her former home, and they were wearing out! Her boots were full of holes! John spent most of his time over at Charley's or Ren's when he wasn't working — they'd drink home brew, and he'd come home late most nights quite inebriated.

In the latter part of January, the children around Love Lake found the ice on the lake just right for sledding and ice-skating. John, Ren and Charley cut ice off the lake to store in the ice-house at the south end of the lake. They'd cover the ice with big heaping piles of sawdust and sell it down at Atlanta later in the year. It was time to cut wood, and the Dennis brothers kept busy cutting wood on their own land, as well as at the McGinnis and Hughs places. John informed Wilmath one day that he had purchased a horse and buggy from old Mr. Van Pelt. He and Ren had put a smokehouse on a bobsled and moved it down the road for Van Pelt, and he was so pleased with the work that he had given John a good deal on the horse and buggy. At least, they had some transportation now!

Spring weather surfaced in April. Mira Dennis came by, along with Ren's wife, Mollie, and helped Wilmath start a small garden out back of the house. There was an abundance of rain that year, and true to John's word, Long Branch did get out down by the Birchs', and he and the other brothers had to spend the night there before coming home the next day. John gave Wilmath the job of feeding the horse, and after caring for the animal and tidying up the house, she spent the rest of her time visiting Emma Corman and her two sisters-in-law.

During the summer, John was home very little. He was putting up hay for Doc Gooding and Dic Davidson until dark each night. Then he drank with his brothers, arriving home quite late. Wilmath was homesick for Ma and the rest of her family, but she had to be content to write letters to them because John had said there was no money for train fare to La Plata.

The fall of 1885 wasn't much different. Cold weather would soon set in again and crops needed gathering. Two days during the week, Wilmath helped Emma Corman, who had a Flowergarden pattern quilt in wooden frames in the sitting room. It was a time to visit and catch up on the news at Love Lake. The two ladies mentioned that, in a couple of months, Mira Dennis would be having a fourth child.

Close to Christmas time, Wilmath was helping Emma bind the quilt that was now almost finished. Emma was making it for a Christmas present for her brother and family, who lived in Kansas City. They talked excitedly about the news of the day — Almira Dennis had just given birth to a baby daughter, Pearl.

"Oh, Wilmath," sighed Emma, "I always wanted a girl. I'll bet Mira's glad she's finally got one after having three boys. Why, there are so many things a woman could teach a daughter!"

"Yes, just think — we'd have an extra pair of hands to help with the quilting!"

Wilmath dreaded Christmas. There was still no money in the Dennis household. John began consuming more liquor, and sometimes he'd be gone overnight. He said he'd just stayed at Charley's or Ren's and "slept it off." She wondered if that was true, but she said nothing. It would have been nice to see Paulina and her brothers and sisters in La Plata at Christmas, but she knew that was not possible.

One day in the middle of February, Wilmath came to help Emma work on another quilt; this time it was a Nine Patch. The day was a cold one, and the ladies stopped quilting after Wilmath had been there about an hour. Emma had gotten the feeling that Wilmath wanted to tell her something from the moment she had first entered the house. Now, as they were drinking some hot tea and relaxing in front of the fire blazing in the fireplace, Wilmath divulged her news to her best friend.

"Em," she started softly, "I think I'm going to have a baby." Emma's eyes lit up — envious of her friend's news, but at the same time feeling genuinely happy for her.

"Oh, Willie, now you won't be so lonely during the day — you'll have the baby for company and to take care of."

"Well, I do worry — we have so little money — I don't know how we'll manage," Wilmath confided.

"You know I'll help you any way I can," Emma assured her.

When Wilmath told John about the forthcoming arrival, he said, "Maybe it'll be a boy — every man wants a boy to work beside him."

"Is that all men think about when they have a child? Why, you're as bad as old John Corman!"

"Willie, you've got to admit he's getting on up in years, and those two boys they've adopted will be a big help to them one of these days."

By March, John had been cutting wood for several months, but money was still scarce. Wilmath's boots had given out a month ago, and she went barefoot most of the time. John had expected her to carry water from the well up to the house in the snow, and the snow was so cold on her bare feet! She almost got them frost-bitten several times! He just didn't seem to care, knowing that she was pregnant and experiencing this hardship.

The usual spring rains came in April. Wilmath was taking care of the horse and had a garden in. She was getting larger as the months went by. John paid little attention to her, and his drinking continued.

Summer started out hot and dry, and by July 1896 the temperatures soared into the mid nineties. The first week of July, Wilmath received a letter from Ma asking her to come to La Plata to have the baby. When Wilmath approached John about the offer, he was agreeable.

"That's fine with me," he said approvingly. "There's not much for you to do around here except take care of the horse, and I'll take him over to Ren's while you are gone. I'll be doin' some extra work for Ketchums, and I'll have the train fare for you by next week."

Wilmath realized that he'd miss her very little. For that matter, she wouldn't miss him much, either. He hadn't shown much interest at all in his unborn child she was carrying. She would miss Mira, Mollie and Emma. They would be good sources of knowledge and would be of great help with the care of the infant when she returned.

On a Monday morning in the middle of July, John put Wilmath on the train at Love Lake. She still had no shoes and was wearing a large dress that had belonged to Mira Dennis when she'd carried Pearl. As she rode on the train, heading north toward La Plata, she felt relieved as she thought of how much more relaxed she'd feel having her baby in her old home, with Ma nearby. I can't believe that this child will ever have much of a life with John Dennis, she thought or, for that matter, would she! She brushed these negative thoughts aside and dropped off for a short nap.

When the train pulled into La Plata, old Pete was sitting in the wagon waiting by the side of the depot to take her home. He looked older and thinner since she'd last seen him.

"Hello, there, Wilmath," he called. "Ma sent me to fetch you." Pete helped her get settled in the seat next to him, and soon she was riding contentedly along beside her stepfather. He was trying to avoid an occasional hole in the dirt road. "Whoa — don't want to have that baby here on the road, do we? From the looks of things, it ain't far away!"

Wilmath smiled, "No, I think you'll have a new grandbaby in a couple of weeks or before." They rode over the railroad tracks, Pete slowing the horses to a walk and then on up the road to the familiar two-story farmhouse. The paint was peeling badly on the wooden structure. Probably Pete hadn't been able to get it painted, and those boys certainly wouldn't be much help!

"Come on in, daughter," Paulina urged, as she stood, arms open wide at the door. "Looks like I'll need to go tell Samantha Jenkins to be ready before long." Samantha served as the neighborhood midwife.

Wilmath felt right at home back in her old room. Amy and Orena had their own room, and Vivian, who had occupied Wilmath's old room since she had left, had been relegated to sleeping on a cot in Amy and Orena's room during her sister's stay with them. Earl and Vic were sleeping on cots in the sitting room.

Wilmath heard little from Love Lake. John had written a postcard only once, and that was to acknowledge the brief card Wilmath had written him to let him know she'd arrived safely at Ma's.

The 25th day of July started off like any other hot dry day, with very little air stirring outside. Wilmath woke up and started the day feeling better than usual. She was downstairs later and was helping Paulina fix lunch when the first stabbing pain hit. It was over quickly, but shortly another pain came on. Throughout the afternoon the pains grew more intense and more frequent. Paulina told Pete to go over to Samantha's and tell her to come on over to the house. In the meantime, she insisted that Wilmath go upstairs to her room and lay down on the bed.

Once there, Wilmath's body was racked with pains that she'd never before experienced! Paulina was downstairs, busily boiling water and gathering up fresh rags when Samantha knocked at the door.

"Howdy, Samantha," Paulina greeted her neighbor, as she

ushered her into the house. “I think Willie’s getting about ready to bring that young ’un into this world.” Samantha hurried up the stairs followed by Paulina. Wilmath, now drenched in sweat and almost out of her mind with the searing pain, felt her mother’s arms around her shoulders.

“Now, listen carefully — I know you’re hurtin’ somethin’ terrible! You’re new at this. Samantha’s here, and we’ll soon have this all over with! You’re built well for havin’ babies, girl — you’re gonna be fine!”

Wilmath felt numbed by the pain. Several times, she heard Samantha’s voice, seemingly from far away, telling her to “bear down.” She was beginning to feel immensely tired from all the pushing, when she heard Samantha say something about one more giant push. Mustering up all of her strength, the young woman pushed with all her might — releasing from her body a new life and at the same time, unburdening herself from the awful pain! Then she heard the boisterous cry of an infant.

“Oh, my, Wilmath, dear,” Paulina said with pride, “you have a precious little daughter.” It felt strange becoming a mother right after that one big push, Wilmath noticed with wonderment.

Samantha cut the cord and washed the baby, then wrapped her in an old white flannel blanket. She handed the child to her mother. A tiny baby with fuzzy light strawberry blonde hair opened its blue eyes for just a moment, then closed them again.

“She’s beautiful,” Wilmath whispered almost to herself. “I thought I’d have a boy — John wanted it to be a boy!”

“Now, you quit worryin’ — every man thinks he wants a boy, but he’ll love his new daughter,” Paulina assured her. Wilmath doubted that John would ever really care about this child, particularly now that it was a girl!

Tired from the birthing of her first child, Wilmath drifted off to sleep, confident that Paulina would tend to the needs of the infant until she could rest her weary body.

A few days later, when her strength returned, she wrote a letter to John.

“We have a darling little baby girl. I named her ‘Lottie Mae.’ I would like to stay here until I’m feeling better, then we’ll be home.”

She had received no reply from her letter. One week later, they heard someone coming up the lane in a buggy. Soon, there was a knock at the door. Pete looked through the screen, and there stood John!

"Hello, Pa," he bellowed. "I've come to take my little family home." Pete beckoned him inside. Wilmath was holding Lottie, trying to recover from the surprise of her husband's unexpected arrival.

"I didn't know you were coming this soon!"

"Well, Willie, things need doin' at the place — my batchin' down there kinda got things in a mess. I figured you'd be up to travelin' by now."

"Aren't you gonna take a look at your new daughter — maybe hold her?"

"Naw, babies are all alike, and you wrote me about her. I'm sure she's fine."

"Now, son," Pete admonished him, "don't be so stubborn about havin' a boy — you got sisters, you know — that means I had daughters."

"Yeah, well, Pa, you had lots of boys, too. You know they're necessary, especially with farmin' and all, and, besides, a man can't take a girl places with him like he can a boy!"

"Nevertheless, I think you should be grateful the Good Lord gave you a fine healthy baby!"

Paulina gathered up a few things for Wilmath and gave her some homemade jelly, bread and meat to take home with her. Pete disappeared and soon came out of the bedroom carrying a brand new pair of ladies' boots.

"Here, Willie," he said, "Ma and me want you to have these — can't have you runnin' around barefoot this winter — why, you'll catch your death of cold! You need to stay healthy to take care of that baby!"

"Thanks, Pa," Wilmath said gratefully, with tears in her eyes.

John had already loaded the things she was taking back to Love Lake in the buggy. She could tell that he was in a hurry to get going. Holding the infant in her arms, she climbed the stairs and peered into the bedroom where her sisters, Amy and Orena, were engrossed in a new game. She gave them both a hug and said good-bye. They each gave their new niece, who was sleeping peacefully, a little kiss on her cheek. Orena, Wilmath thought, looked a little peaked, but the little seven-year-old girl was gazing lovingly at little Lottie. Wilmath went downstairs and poked her head into the kitchen, bidding a fond farewell to 12-year-old Vivian, who was doing the dishes.

"Thanks for everything, Ma," she said, as she hugged Paulina. "Tell the boys good-bye for me, too." Pa had sent Earl and Vic out to the field earlier in the day to chop thistles. Pete held the door open for the new mother, who was carrying her infant daughter. She reached up to him, planting a kiss on his old weathered wrinkled cheek and whispered quickly in his ear, "Thanks again for the boots."

John by now had lost all patience and was yelling loudly, "Come on, Willie — let's get a move on." She and little Lottie climbed into the buggy, and off they went down the dusty lane. Wilmath had little to say. She had her baby snuggled close to her breast and dreaded returning to Love Lake. Maybe things will be better now that I have Lottie, she thought — a faint hope rising in her heart!

CHAPTER THREE

JOHN, WILMATH AND LOTTIE arrived at Love Lake in the early afternoon. On the way there, John had enlightened Wilmath on the happenings that had transpired while she was in La Plata. John's mother, Martha, had gotten a divorce from William Penrod and had come to Love Lake to build a house on her property that she had inherited from the Reids. She had been staying with Charley and Mira, while the Dennis boys — John, Charley, and Ren — had been working on the dwelling for their mother. Even Seba had been helping on the project when he could get a free moment. Wilmath thought about Martha — she had her quirks all right, but the tall, thin, bird-like woman treated Wilmath well. It seemed strange to have Pete Dennis' first wife as a mother-in-law. However, it had blossomed into a close relationship.

They pulled up to their house, and Wilmath, carrying the baby who was wide awake and crying now, walked to the door and entered the house. It was an amazing sight! Everything was tidily in place. All the dishes were done, the laundry was neatly folded in a pile on the trunk, and there was a bouquet of wild roses in an old blue fruit jar sitting on the kitchen table. By the bed, sitting in one corner of the sitting room, was a small, handmade wooden cradle.

"Oh, my!" she gasped. "What on earth? Who did all this?"

"I have no idea, Willie. It was a mess when I came for you. I was dreadin' you seein' the place — thought you'd be madder'n a hornet when you saw the shape it was in!"

"Well, I just can't believe ..." her voice trailed off as she looked around, taking in every part of the tiny house. She walked over to the cradle, bent down and looked at it. Someone had done a splendid job building it. Turning the cradle upside down, she read the initials that were carved on the bottom: “S.S.D.” Smiling to herself, she thought — I should have known — only Seba would have been that thoughtful! He was so special — her stepbrother and childhood companion. She said nothing to John and laid Lottie in her new bed and started fixing supper, thanks to the generous offering of food Ma had sent.

After supper she nursed Lottie, then climbed into bed, tired from the ride. John was asleep already. I'll find out who made our homecoming so special tomorrow, she vowed, as sleep came upon her, too.

John was up early, ready to go help work on Martha Penrod's house. They hoped to have it done by October before cold weather set in. Later in the morning as Wilmath was putting a few things away while Lottie slept, she heard voices outside and then a knock at the door. She opened it and was greeted warmly by Mira, Martha, Mollie and her friend, Emma.

“We're so glad you're back, Willie,” Emma said, as she hugged her friend. “We've come to see Lottie.” They could see that the baby was sound asleep in the cradle.

“I came to see my new granddaughter,” Martha exclaimed, as she gave her daughter-in-law a kiss. “Perhaps I could hold her.”

“Maybe she will be awake before long,” chorused Mira and Mollie.

“I'll fix us some tea and we'll chat a bit, and maybe by then she'll be awake,” Wilmath suggested. She was so happy to see these friendly faces once again. “Tell me all the news — I understand you're moving up here and will soon have a new house, Mother Penrod.”

“Yes, you know, I just would be rattling around by myself in the old home place at Cherry Box. Did John tell you about poor Daniel? He hadn't been himself since he and the other boys drilled that well over in Shelby County last year, and he got hit hard on his head. Well, he went plumb loco — he got so violent that we had to commit him to the asylum at St. Joe. The bad thing is that it's such a long way to go to see him — we have to take the train clear down to Carrollton, and once we arrive there, we have to board an excursion boat up the river to St. Joseph.”

“I think Charley said somethin' about him and the other brothers goin' up there in September, when they have special excursion rates from Carrollton to St. Joe," Mira added.

"What will you do with the home place then, Martha?" Wilmath asked.

"Oh, Seba's gonna live there while the boys are buildin' my house. Then after that I may rent it out. You know Seba — he's sort of a wanderer — don't stay in one place too long — always wants to be on the go — moves here and there." Wilmath smiled as she heard Martha describe the elusive Seba. Then she thought about the surprisingly clean condition she found the house in yesterday.

"Say — I wonder if any of you know who could have cleaned my house and fixed it so nice for my homecoming yesterday?" she inquired. All four ladies smiled shyly.

"Well, it was a joint effort," Mira replied. "Martha wanted to have things nice for you, and Mollie and I agreed, and Emma said she'd help. We all pitched in yesterday morning and had it done in no time at all."

"Thank you so much," Wilmath said gratefully. "You have no idea what it meant to me and Lottie." She looked at the infant wiggling in the cradle — eyes open now. "I know that Seba made her cradle."

"Yes," admitted Martha, "it was all his idea — he said that the little one would be needin' a place to sleep." Wilmath promised herself that she'd thank Seba the very next time she saw him. Each of the ladies took turns holding Lottie and admiring the tiny infant.

"I think it best that we go home for now. If you need our help, just let us know," Martha offered, with the other three ladies in agreement. As they went out the door, Wilmath felt thankful for their friendship and companionship — it was the only bright spot in her life besides Lottie.

She spent most of her time the rest of the summer tending what was left of the small garden, feeding the horse, fixing John's meals and taking care of the household chores and caring for Lottie. John was helping farmers and, in between, helping on his mother's house.

Fall was coming to Love Lake. Temperatures were cooler — Wilmath had to put heavier blankets on the bed. She developed a cough and it persisted. Charley Dennis had brought by some sarsaparilla, telling her he had recently switched from Kennedy's brand to Hood's. Another week passed, and Wilmath knew that her lungs were congested.

One day late in September, Mira came by and insisted on driving Wilmath down to Atlanta to the doctor. They'd drop Lottie off at Mollie's on the way. Arriving in Atlanta, they went directly to Dr. Thompson's office, which was upstairs over Thompson and Atteberry's Drug Store. A sign outside read: "Dr. J. Thompson — Physician and Surgeon — Special attention given to chronic diseases." After a brief examination, the doctor told Wilmath that she had pneumonia.

"Young lady," he said, "you go home and take to your bed for a couple of weeks."

"Oh, I couldn't possibly do that — what with all the work and Lottie," Wilmath insisted hoarsely.

"Now, Willie, we'll manage," soothed Mira.

Mira took Lottie home with her, after assuring Wilmath that she and Martha would take good care of the child, and Wilmath went to bed. Emma Corman brought over a bottle of Ballard's Horehound Syrup, thinking it might help. Mollie fixed several meals and brought to the house for John and Wilmath. It was good to know that she had relatives and a friend who were so helpful and thoughtful.

On the last day of September, John came home with some bad news. "Willie, we went down to the mill in Atlanta today — Will Daugherty'd just come down from La Plata, and he had a message for you from your ma. Orena's done passed away."

Shock filtered through the sick woman's body. "Oh, what can I do? I'm sick here abed! What caused her death, did he say?"

"Well, 'nears I can tell, she'd been havin' pains in her side, and by the time old Doc Gates got out there, her appendix had done busted, infection set in, and she died."

"Oh, if I was only well enough, I could be there for Ma," she lamented.

"I'm goin' on up there and see what I can do. Pa'll be wantin' to have some help with the burial. When I was first married, they was sellin' lots in La Plata Cemetery fairly cheap, and I got me one. Reckon I could ask Pa if he wants to put Orena in there." Wilmath lay back on her pillow. How sad that a life should end at seven years old!

By the third week of October, Wilmath was up and about.

She was still weak, but she was caring for Lottie. The house was full of cracks — cold air was pouring in. She began stuffing some rags in them, trying to keep out the chilly wind. Martha Penrod's house was almost done. Wilmath had hoped to be well enough to go down and see the new structure. She had also hoped Seba would still be there working, as she'd not had a chance to thank him for the baby's cradle.

Mira came by a week before Thanksgiving and said that they were having a family dinner at her house. "Mother Penrod hasn't quite gotten everything in order in the new house, so we'll be having the dinner." What a big dinner it was! There was turkey, sweet potatoes, gooseberry pie, Lady Baltimore cake and cranberries, plus several other dishes. Rosie and Frank Thorn came from Edina; Seba came, bringing his grandma, Phoebe Reid, from Cherry Box; and Ren and Mollie and Charley and Mira and children were there. In the afternoon Frank Thorn got out his fiddle and played "In the Sweet Bye and Bye." Before the song was over, Wilmath noticed that Seba had gone out on the back porch, and she slipped quietly out to join him.

"You know, I never got a chance to thank you for that cradle you made for Lottie," Wilmath said softly, as she stood by the porch railing.

"Wilmath, dear, did you like it? She's a darling little girl," he remarked, with a smile on his handsome face. "When she was stayin' with Mother and Mira while you were sick, I would stop by often and hold her," he admitted.

"Oh, did you, Seba? How kind of you!"

"Well, she's my niece, and, besides — she's yours, too," he said affectionately. Wilmath's heart was thumping rapidly. He hasn't forgotten how close we always were, she thought.

Aloud, she said, "Seba, where you gonna go now that Martha's house is almost done?"

"Oh, you know me — I can't seem to stay in one place too long. I've been stayin' at Mother's house in Cherry Box, but Frank and Rosie want me to come live in a house near theirs at Edina."

"It's getting cold out here," shuddered Wilmath. "I don't want to get sick again — maybe I should go in."

"Wilmath," he said, as he put his hand in hers, "if you ever need me for anything, anytime, please come to me." She looked into his blue eyes and was overwhelmed with his offer. There was a closeness she felt with this man that she'd never experienced with anyone else before. A tear traveled slowly down to rest on her cheek. She nodded her head affirmatively, and they made their way back into the house to join the others.

Christmas was nearing, and the temperatures were dropping each day. It seemed that John wasn't home much now, even though he was no longer working on Martha's house. There was little money, too. Some days when it was bitterly cold, Wilmath took little Lottie and went to bed and covered up to keep warm.

One day when the weather was better than average for that time of year, Martha, Mira and Emma came by Wilmath's and announced that they were all taking the train down to Atlanta to do some Christmas shopping. They wanted Willie and Lottie to come with them. Mollie had stayed home with her three nephews and Pearl.

"I don't have a cent — even for the train fare," Wilmath admitted sadly.

"Child, I'll take care of that — now get ready, we're going!" declared Martha. Wilmath put on her best dress, bundled Lottie up tightly and went out the door with the other three women.

Once on the train, they discussed their shopping plans. Martha wanted to look at sewing machines, and Mira needed some new lamps. Wilmath remained silent, as she knew she couldn't afford to buy anything. When they arrived in Atlanta, they headed immediately to Johnston and Turner's Hardware Store. They had some lamps advertised that Mira wanted to buy. Martha Penrod was looking at a New Home treadle sewing machine she'd seen in the ad in the "Atlanta News." She was in the process of buying the machine when she saw Wilmath sitting on a chair, holding Lottie, looking forlorn.

"Just a minute," she told Abner Johnston, "I'll be right back."

"Wilmath — listen," Martha said, as she pressed some money into the young woman's hand, "why don't you go across the street to Trilby's Photo Company and get your picture taken with Lottie? You can order several to give for Christmas gifts. After all, I need a picture of my new granddaughter!" Wilmath had worn her good dress, and, she thought, I might as well accept the offer.

"All right — thank you, Mother Penrod — we'll be back here soon." Emma, who had just come from buying some quilt material at the dry goods store, offered to accompany Wilmath to the photographer's to help her with Lottie.

On the way home, the tired women were discussing their purchases. The hardware store would send the sewing machine and lamps up to Love Lake in about a week. Wilmath told them that Trilby's would mail the photos to her right before Christmas. Emma Corman was planning to put another quilt in the frames after Christmas to while away the long winter months. This time, she informed the others, she was making a Necktie pattern quilt.

John was spending most of the days before Christmas cutting wood and drinking with Charley and Ren. A long letter arrived for Wilmath from Paulina the day before Christmas. She mentioned that the holiday would be a sad occasion without little Orena there. Wilmath wished she was at Ma's — life with John was not working out. She didn't want to live this way the rest of her life. John paid little attention to her and Lottie. He didn't seem to care about doing anything around home. Seba wouldn't have treated her like this, she thought. Just thinking of Seba somehow made Wilmath feel better.

Martha Penrod had Christmas dinner at her new home. Wilmath was disappointed to find out that Seba would not be there. She had decided to give him one of the photos she'd had taken at Trilby's; now, she would have to mail it to Edina. Martha announced that Grandma Reid would be coming to live with her in the new house before New Year's. Both ladies were alone, and since Seba wouldn't be living in Cherry Box any longer, there would be no one to look in on Grandma Reid. Martha served a sumptuous meal. Mollie and Ren, Charley and Mira and children, and John, Wilmath and Lottie were the only family members present. Seba had gone to Grandma Reid's house in Cherry Box with the Thorns for Christmas. Afterward, they were going to help the elderly lady pack her possessions, so that she could move to Love Lake.

New Year's Day, the Dennis brothers chopped wood all day on the 20 acres back of Martha Penrod's house. In the evening, the family gathered at Martha's to have an oyster supper for Grandma Reid. Wilmath said very little, as she listened to the brothers talk about the news they'd gathered a few days before. They went to the mill at Atlanta on Saturdays, where all of

Cherry Box and Leonard came to trade. Ren mentioned that he was clearing timber, and Charles added that he heard that there was going to be a new saw mill south on Long Branch over by Ketchum's. John joined in and said that a new iron bridge was being built across East Fork, by John Saling's. Mira was telling the women that Will Parsons was boarding with them this winter, as he'd bought the McGinnis 40 from them.

"It's a good thing Harley Reardon isn't gonna be stayin' with us now," she said. "He's back up near La Plata with his cousin, Fred Milford, and workin' on Joe Daugherty's place."

Martha mentioned that she had attended a revival at the Atlanta Baptist Church, and that there were 12 additions and several conversions.

What does all this matter, Wilmath thought — she was going back to Ma's!

CHAPTER FOUR

JANUARY 20, 1897, John put Wilmath and Lottie on the Wabash at Love Lake. The husband and wife had little to say to one another. He had borrowed the money for the train fare from Martha Penrod.

As they rode north toward La Plata, Wilmath decided that the only ones she would be leaving behind and would truly miss would be Mira, Mollie, Martha and Emma.

When she got to the La Plata depot, she walked toward the livery stable. They would know there if anyone in town would be going out northeast toward the folks' place. Luckily, Doc Gates had a call to make at Wilson Town, and he was just getting in his buggy as Wilmath and Lottie neared the stable.

"Hey, Doc," she shouted, "I hear you're goin' near the home place — can we have a ride?"

"Why, of course — oh, Wilmath, how are you?" the old doctor asked, finally recognizing her.

"Fine — we're just goin' down to visit Pete and Ma for awhile," she explained. She added no more to the conversation, and they climbed up to sit beside him.

As they arrived at the Dennis house, tears welled up in Wilmath's eyes as she thought, I'll have a lot of explainin' to do to Ma.

Pete and Paulina were indeed surprised to see Wilmath and the baby, as they got out of the conveyance and waved at Dr. Gates who was now making his way back down the lane.

"Willie, we didn't expect you, child. What on earth are you and that baby doin' out in this cold weather?" Paulina inquired, as they were admitted into the house, shutting out the cold weather.

"Well, Ma," she began, "my marriage to John is over!"

"Don't talk like that — everybody has troubles one time or another."

"You just don't understand. He wasn't hardly ever home, he didn't pay no attention to Lottie or me, and we have no money. He's been drinkin' that whiskey with those brothers of his almost every night." Wilmath started to say more, then she suddenly remembered that John was, after all, Pete's son.

Paulina made them sit by the black pot-bellied stove in the sitting room. The warmth felt good — not only from the stove, but also from being near her family, Wilmath thought contentedly.

"What're you gonna do now, girl?" Ma wanted to know, later in the day.

"I haven't any plans. I know that I never want to live with John Dennis again!"

Wilmath heard nothing from John. Occasionally, word drifted down from Daugherty's of happenings at Love Lake. Ma kept trying to get her to write to John or try to restart her married life.

Just before spring arrived, Paulina took her daughter aside. "I have news," she said in hushed tones, "I'm goin' to have another baby." Wilmath could hardly believe the words that were coming out of her mother's mouth! Ma was close to 40 years old, and she'd already had six kids — this would be number seven!

"Oh, Ma," she said, visibly upset, "you're so tied down now, and Pete is 64. He's an old man. You can't be happy about this!"

"Think of it this way, it may be God's way of givin' me another child, since Orena's gone," Paulina surmised sadly. "Not that any child could ever be replaced," she added. Wilmath said no more, but was still somewhat ruffled by her mother's revelation.

One day in the middle of July, Charley Dennis came to La Plata to help Pa with the hay. He'd just finished helping Doc Gooding with his hay the day before. At supper that evening, he announced that he and Harley Reardon were going into the gate business together in a couple of months. He told them that Seba was still in Edina, living in town and helping Frank Thorn on his farm there.

Before retiring that evening, Charley took Wilmath aside. "Listen, Willie," he said quietly, "you better do somethin' about that brother of mine — you need to move back to Love Lake."

"What do you mean?" she asked curiously.

Charley continued, "He's keepin' company with that little Hampton divorcee up there across the lake." Wilmath vaguely remembered who he was talking about. Fannie Hampton lived clear across the lake, southeast of John's place. She'd seen her several times at the general store. Fannie was a tiny little woman, and she walked with a limp.

"I really don't care what John's doin'," she told Charles, "I'm not comin' back. Perhaps that is why he was never home!"

In October Paulina had a new baby. She was a blonde-haired little girl, and Pete and Paulina named her Sylvia. Wilmath helped with the cooking, laundry and the care of little Sylvia.

A week later, she was so engrossed in her duties that she hadn't even paid attention to who was at the door. She heard Pete saying, "Well, son, 'bout time you came 'round." She instantly knew who her stepfather was talking to.

John Dennis made his way into the kitchen where she was heating water for doing dishes.

"Hi, there, Willie — how've you been? Ready to come back home yet?" he asked loudly. She could tell by the smell of him that he'd been drinking. Saying nothing, she poured the boiling water into the dishpan. "Oh, come on now — is that any way to treat your husband?" he demanded.

"John," she said calmly, "I'm not goin' back to Love Lake with you now or any other time."

"Oh, is that so? Well, I'm still your husband, ain't I, and if I say you're goin', you are!"

"No," she said with staunch firmness, "I'm not. Besides, I hear you have an interest in someone else. Fannie Hampton, isn't it?"

"Let's not bring her into this," John said, his voice growing louder by the minute.

Pete had come into the kitchen, his eyes staring straight at his son. "Now listen, son, we aren't havin' loud arguin' around this house. I'd hoped that Willie'd see fit to try again with you, but bein's how she's set her head differently, I guess you better go on back by yourself."

John grabbed his old tattered hat and stalked out the door, slamming it loudly!

CHAPTER FIVE

A FEW WEEKS after Sylvia's birth, Paulina was feeling better and able to do most of her work. She thought that Wilmath looked tired from trying to keep up with all the kids and doing the household duties.

"Dear, why don't you go to Edina and visit Frank and Rosie for a few days? They don't have any kids up there, and I think you need some peace and quiet after all you've done here. Lottie can stay with me — Vivian will help me with her and the baby."

The following Tuesday Wilmath boarded the Wabash at La Plata and rode to the new depot in Kirksville. She had to wait there about 30 minutes before boarding the OK Railroad that would take her east to Edina. The new structure was certainly an improvement over the former depot. It was twice as large and sported a turret on top of the building that was shaped like a gazebo. The building was steeped in Victorian architecture.

When she reached the depot in Edina, she expected to see the Thorns waiting for her. In a few minutes, she heard a familiar voice.

"Wilmath!" She could feel her heart leap — she'd know that voice anywhere!

"Oh, Seba," she smiled, "I didn't expect you."

"Frank and Rosie wanted me to come for you. We're going to drive out to the farm — I've brought their horse and buggy. It's not very far out of town." When he had gotten her settled in the buggy, he continued. "They are starting to get the crops in now."

He was such a good-looking man — with twinkling eyes — so gay and full of humor!

When they arrived at the Thorns', Rosie and Frank had just

come in from the field.

"We're so glad you've come," Rosie said graciously as they went inside the house. Their home was neat, tidy and, most of all, quiet. Maybe it was a good thing Rosie couldn't have children — they had more money to buy nice things, Wilmath decided.

Rosie had gone to the dry goods store in Edina before her stepsister had arrived, and she had purchased some quality material and a Butterick pattern and had made a new dress for Wilmath. When she saw Rosie's creation, Wilmath was speechless! What a kind thing she had done!

Wilmath liked clothes, though she had few. That will change one day, she thought. Rosie had an old hat that still looked fashionable. She insisted Wilmath try it on and keep it if she liked it. Why, she liked it just fine! In fact, she looked like a real lady now. She peered into Rosie's looking glass, adjusting the hat first one way and then another. Yessiree!! A hat was just the right finishing touch! Then, glancing at the array of cosmetics on Rosie's dresser, she spotted a can of lilac-scented talcum powder. Now that she was a lady, it was high time she was usin' some of that good-smellin' stuff! She saw a big powder puff lying in a pretty glass tray, and sprinkling some talc on the puff, she powdered her neck and upper torso with the fragrant scent. She'd always savored the aroma of lilacs!

The following day, Rosie announced that she and Frank needed to go to Frank's brother Robert's farm in Shelby County for a couple of days. Frank was helping gather the crops, and she was helping her sister-in-law with the cooking for the hands.

"Would you like to go with us, Willie? If not, you can stay here until we get back. It's close enough, you could even walk into town during the day if you wanted to."

"Thanks, Rosie, I think I'll stay here. I'll straighten up the house for you and find something to do." The next afternoon, after finishing the housecleaning, Wilmath decided to walk in to town. She donned her new dress and hat, put a dash of that talc on and made her way towards town. It took about 45 minutes to walk to Edina's business district. She looked in the windows of the stores along the main street, then went over near the square to sit on a bench to rest.

The square was an empty piece of ground, edged with trees — the old courthouse had burned on Christmas Eve, 1885. Although arson was suspected, no one was ever apprehended. Knox County business had been conducted in a building on Lafayette Street ever since the county courthouse had burnt down.

Suddenly, Wilmath felt someone tap her on the shoulder — she looked up to see Seba standing by the bench. Then he sat down beside her.

"Wilmath, what're you doin' in town all by yourself — where's Rosie?" She explained the whereabouts of her host and hostess to him. Then he asked, "When's the last time you've eaten today?"

She hadn't given it a thought — she hadn't eaten a thing since breakfast! And now it was already well after noon!

"Would you like to come to my house, and I'll fix you a bite to eat, and we can visit?"

"I guess that'd be okay," she agreed. She got up off the bench and followed her stepbrother as they walked south on Main Street. They had gone that direction about two blocks when they turned west on Oak Street. When they came to the second house on the south side of the street, he gestured toward a walk leading up to a small, but neat, two-room house facing north on Oak. As she stepped through the door he was holding ajar for her, she noticed that the place was surprisingly clean for a bachelor's house.

"Here's where I'm hangin' my hat these days, at least for now," he informed her. "Frank and Rosie own this place — they lived here before they moved to the farm at the edge of town. It isn't much, but it's all I need for awhile."

"Seba, you're so different from the rest of your family — you really take care of what possessions you have," she complimented him, meaning every word of it. The furnishings were meager, but they included the items necessary for him to carry on his daily life.

Seba busied himself preparing lunch for them, while Wilmath looked about. A small bedroom adjoined the kitchen. The kitchen contained a table, three odd chairs and an old wood cook stove. A wash basin stood near the door, where a bucket of drinking water and dipper sat also. She peeked into the door that led to the bedroom. An old upholstered loveseat sat in one corner of the room with a table close by. In another corner was a three-quarter wood-framed bed with a feather tick on it, a worn quilt covering it. Flour-sack pillowcases covered the feather pillows at the top of the bed. She spied an old camel-backed trunk at the foot of the bed — the lid open just wide enough for her to see that here was where he kept his books, magazines and newspapers. He loved to read, because he had often told her of the places he read about, far away from here.

"Let's sit down and eat — we need to hurry — it gets darker now that fall is here," he said invitingly. He had spread a large flour sack on the table and set two places for them. She discovered that she was really very hungry by now!

"Um — um," she said, as she tasted some biscuits topped with butter and blackberry jelly.

"Mother gave me several jars of jelly. The blackberries grow wild up there in the woods behind her house, and they are so very nice and large. Rosie keeps me supplied with fresh biscuits and plenty of butter." His sister had also given him some "fried down" sausage cakes that he'd quickly warmed for them in an old iron skillet.

Wilmath noticed a Seth Thomas clock sitting on a wooden mantle on the kitchen wall. It was ticking loudly and bonged once on the half hour and struck the appropriate number of strikes on each hour. It had just this minute struck five times, indicating that it was five o'clock. The sun was beginning to set, and she realized that it would be dark soon.

"I must be going before long," she informed him regretfully. "Rosie and Frank won't be back to the farm until sometime tomorrow, but I want to get there before it gets any later."

Seba said nothing. He was looking across the table at the pretty woman. How different things might be if she wasn't his brother's wife! Wilmath had always been special to him — she always would be! It broke his heart to see how cold John had acted toward his young bride. She deserved a better life.

Aloud, he said thoughtfully, " Perhaps before you go you might like to pick out a book or magazine to take with you. I don't want you out there walkin' in the dark alone. As soon as you decide on somethin' to read, I'll walk out there with you."

He took her hand and led her into the adjoining room. He pushed the old trunk lid all the way open, revealing dozens of magazines, papers and several books. Wilmath bent down to sort through his collection. He stared intently at the form standing before him. Her tall straight body was angled so that her large breasts strained against the soft material of the bodice of her new dress. Her waist, he noticed, was tiny in proportion to the rest of her body — her stomach held flat by her staved corset. At 17, she showed little evidence of bearing a child a year earlier. Seba, too, bent down — his body towering over hers, as he offered to help her with her selection. He got a whiff of her powder — it was the fragrant scent of lilacs!

Wilmath became very aware of his closeness now. His hand folded over hers — that soft, loving hand she'd first held over at Pa's crick. The two straightened their bodies and turned away from the trunk, their eyes meeting, words being insignificant. Sensuous feelings washed over their bodies from head to toe. Outside, darkness had enveloped the night; neither of them seemed to notice.

They walked the few steps necessary to reach the bed and lie down beside each other. Gradually the garments of each made their way to the floor, until they were only covered by scant underclothes. Still, no words were uttered — the language of love spoke loud and clear. Discarding the final coverings of their bodies, they moved so that they were facing one another, their bodies close together. He showered her with kisses, first on her lips, and then on downward, touching places that made her ache with a desire she'd never known before. She pressed closer to him now, responding to every movement of his body, until they were of one accord, their thoughts centered on one common goal. Suddenly, neither of them could tell which body was theirs — it was if they were both molded into one solid mass of heavenly pleasure!

Afterward, while encircled in Seba's long arms, Wilmath looked at the sleeping man and thought to herself, I'm with the only man I'll ever truly love — even if it's only for one night. I'll remember it forever! Tonight, he's mine — all mine! Then, drowsiness overtook her, and the two young lovers slept quietly through the night — the only sound being the occasional striking of the Seth Thomas on the kitchen shelf.

CHAPTER SIX

IT WAS OVER TWO MONTHS before she saw Seba again. Christmas was coming, and Wilmath had to help Paulina prepare for a huge family dinner. All the Dennis boys and their families would be there, as well as Frank and Rosie Thorn. It would be quite a bunch of people to cook for! On top of that, John Dennis would be coming. Wilmath dreaded that!

Christmas Day arrived, and Wilmath awakened early, got Lottie and Sylvia dressed and went down to the kitchen to help her mother start the cooking for the day. Paulina was already at work as usual. Wilmath suddenly felt nauseated, as the odors of the food cooking on the old wood stove were wafting into the room. In about 20 minutes she bolted out the door, giving her churning stomach its way. When she returned to the kitchen, Paulina noticed the pale look on her daughter's face.

"My goodness, girl, are you ill?"

"No, I don't think so — I just all of a sudden got sick at my stomach!"

"Well, let's hope it's nothin' serious, this bein' Christmas and all." The women worked side by side, assisted by Vivian and Amy, with little Lottie and Sylvia underfoot. Gradually all the Dennis family began pouring in — Charley and Mira and their four children, Mollie and Ren, and John. Then Frank and Rosie and Seba arrived. Seba promptly devoted his attention to Lottie and Sylvia, playfully getting them out of the way of those working in the kitchen. He would make a wonderful father, thought Wilmath, as she watched him tickling and teasing the little girls.

Talk at the table covered several topics. News around Love Lake, Edina and La Plata was discussed. Charley told them he had eight cords of eight-foot wood on his woodpile and had sold and delivered 22 cords to Atlanta and had more to haul. He was getting from a dollar to a dollar and a half per cord. Ren and John said they had 14 acres of wood to cut on the McGinnis place.

Wilmath interrupted the men's talk to ask about Martha Penrod and Grandma Reid. She learned that Martha's brother, Sil Reid, from Sedalia, was up at Love Lake having Christmas dinner with his sister and mother.

The brothers then continued their newsy discussion. Sila Doggett had sold out and bought the Brannans' 60 acres for $600. Charley told Seba that he had butchered the fattest hog he'd ever seen — it weighed 466 pounds, and they got 14 gallons of lard out of it!

Then, talk turned to politics. Although the presidential election was almost two years away, the Dennis family and all of Macon County had hoped to elect William Jennings Bryan to the presidency. He had failed to win during the election in 1896, when McKinley became president. Bryan had come to Macon, the county seat of Macon County, riding in on the Wabash, making speeches, knowing that most of the population of the county were "yellow dog" democrats. Both President McKinley and Bryan gave strong indications that, once again, they planned to oppose each other in the election of 1900.

"I think that Bryan will definitely be president in 1900," Seba predicted. "I know I'm going to vote for him!" They all agreed that Bryan was the candidate of their choice.

After dinner, John cornered Wilmath at one end of the sitting room and asked her to return to Love Lake with him.

"No, I don't think I should do that," she told him emphatically. Pete and Paulina came into the room then and seemed to support John's request.

"Dear, we think you should go — give it another try. After all, you two have Lottie to think about now," Paulina insisted. Wilmath sensed that they had been discussing this situation previously, maybe even with John, because now they were all in agreement that she should give the marriage another try.

Wearily, she gave up and said, "Okay, I guess I've been here underfoot long enough. Maybe I should try once more to make a home of my own." She went to get Lottie, who was thoroughly enjoying the company of her little Aunt Sylvia.

While they were talking, the Thorns and Seba were departing for Edina. Wilmath had no chance to speak to Seba that day with so many people around. Hasty good-byes were said, and only those bound for Love Lake were left to say their farewells.

John, Wilmath and Lottie left for Love Lake. The December afternoon was cold, but there were several old blankets in the buggy to use for cover. Silence prevailed all the way home. Charley and Mira and their children and Mollie and Ren were following in their wagons. Wilmath thought that things were definitely going to have to change if this marriage worked, but doubts were already heavily clouding her mind.

Her doubts proved to be right. During the month she'd been there, she'd cleaned the old house, cooked, done laundry and cared for Lottie. She had been glad to see Martha Penrod, Grandma Reid and Emma Corman, but John stayed away most of the time — even at night. He never explained where he had been. He didn't have to — all of Love Lake was buzzing with the rumors of him being in the constant company of Fannie Hampton. Wilmath wasn't much concerned. At least, he never expected anything romantic from her. It would have paled in comparison to the night she had spent with Seba last fall. Those thoughts of Seba were about the only thing that kept her sane these days. And she really didn't feel well! The nauseated feeling she'd had at Ma's at Christmas hadn't gone away. Even though she hadn't wanted much to eat, it looked like her flat stomach was getting rounder and fuller each morning when she laced up her corset.

One day she mentioned the subject to Mira, who immediately gave her sister-in-law the answer to her current "health" problem.

"Willie, do you suppose you could have another baby on the way?"

"Why, Mira, I wouldn't think so," she replied, too quickly.

"Well, you know, Lottie's two — maybe you're ready to add to your family." Wilmath suddenly felt very ill — not just from the nausea, but from a stabbing and knowing feeling that was evolving from a memory of that night in Edina. Maybe it is true, she thought!

Aloud, she said, "Mira, you could be right — maybe that explains why I've been feelin' under the weather for a while."

"I'm surprised you didn't figure that out, since you've had a baby already!"

"I was never sick like this with Lottie, Mira. I should have known though!"

"I'll bet John will be surprised — maybe this time he'll get that boy he's always wanted!"

"Listen, Mira, I'm going to have to ask you to promise to keep this a secret for awhile. I'm not tellin' John — I've been thinkin' about this marriage and about the fact he's hardly ever here any more, and I've decided I'm goin' back to Ma's, and this time, I'm not EVER comin' back!!"

"I hate to hear that, Wilmath, but I know you've been terribly unhappy, and everyone knows about John and that Hampton woman! You poor girl!"

"I'll miss you, Mira, but I can't live like this. I'm leavin' John a note — would you take me and Lottie to the train tomorrow?"

"Of course, you know I'd do anything for you, Willie." The two women embraced, and they agreed that Mira would pick her sister-in-law and niece up the following morning in the wagon and take them to catch the train to La Plata.

John Dennis didn't come home that night, much to Wilmath's relief. The next day, after leaving a note of good-bye on the kitchen table, Wilmath closed the door to her home and to her marriage.

Paulina and Pete were mildly surprised to see Wilmath and Lottie back so soon. They had hoped the marriage would work out, but they decided to say no more about a reconciliation, as they, too, had heard that John was spending most of his time at "that woman's house on the south side of the lake."

By May Wilmath could no longer conceal her large stomach beneath her clothing. She was forced to tell Ma about the new baby that would arrive in the household in two months. It came as no surprise to her mother, as Paulina, who had birthed seven children herself, had already noticed the changes in her daughter's physical appearance.

"I thought you might be with child," she admitted when Wilmath told her.

"Ma, look, I don't want you to say anything about this to John."

"Dear, he's got to know — he's still your husband!"

"He never wanted Lottie, and, besides, our marriage is over. He's got someone else he's interested in, and the only thing we need to talk about is a divorce."

"He's comin' here in a week or so to help Pa do some plantin'

— you need to talk to him then."

"Yes, I'll do that and get this over with."

"I think you should wait until the child is born before you get a divorce."

Wilmath nodded, "I'm sure he'll agree to that."

She was right! She discussed the situation with John soon after he arrived at La Plata.

"Well, Willie, look at you — getting kind of big, aren't you?" he said as he eyed her. "If I didn't know better, I'd say you're in the family way."

"John, I am. The baby's comin' sometime after the Fourth of July."

"You don't say," he sneered. "Wonder who the father is — we know I'm not, don't we now?"

"I think it's not your concern."

"Oh, really — I'm still your husband. And I was comin' to talk to you about that very thing. Now this makes it all the better — we can make a deal!"

"What are you getting at?" she demanded.

"I need a divorce quickly. Fannie is — ah — also havin' a baby. I want to marry her, and the sooner the better. Now apparently you'll be needin' a father for your baby. If you'll agree to a quick divorce, we'll just say this one here is ours and get the divorce and go on."

"That suits me fine. I was going to ask for a divorce, but I wanted to wait until after the child was born. Would you agree to that?"

"We can start proceedings before long — the divorce won't be granted until the November term of court here in La Plata. Your baby will be two months old by then, and I will be free to marry Fannie. To let you save face, I'll let you be the petitioner. You can make me out to be the culprit — I really don't care."

"Then, it's settled. I'll go to La Plata and see a lawyer soon," she agreed.

CHAPTER SEVEN

ON A WARM, SULTRY 10TH OF JULY 1898, Wilmath gave birth to a baby boy. I'll name him James, she thought — James Dennis — that's his real last name — even though he's Seba's.

Her thoughts traveled back to the past, thinking of her sweet Seba. His thinking seemed to be centered on worldly matters. She remembered how interested he was in politics, wanting William Jennings Bryan to become the next president. That was it! She would name the baby James Bryan Dennis — that would make Seba proud! What would he think, now that he was a father! She'd be free to marry him in a couple of months, and they could be together now as a family.

A week later, Wilmath went to La Plata to the law office of Davis and Overstreet. They agreed to draw up the necessary divorce papers for her. The case would be heard in the November term. The issue of support was addressed, stating in the papers that the two children born of the marriage, "Lottie Mae, age two, and a boy, about two months old," were to receive monetary help from John Dennis. Wilmath doubted that she'd ever collect a cent from him, since he'd never had any money during their marriage. Also, he would be starting a new family with Fannie.

Christmas, 1898, was not a big occasion at the Dennis household. Pete was failing physically. John had married Fannie the first of December and was still living at Love Lake. Charley and Mira were staying at home during Christmas because their children had come down with the chickenpox. Ren and Mollie were going to have dinner with Martha Penrod and Grandma Reid, and Seba and the Thorns were going to Love Lake to be with their mother and grandmother.

Wilmath had written to Seba at Edina, telling him that she needed to talk to him. He wrote back and told her he was going to Oklahoma right after Christmas. He had heard that people from Missouri were going to Oklahoma Territory to settle, and he wanted to keep his eye on the land in the Cherokee Strip in the northern part of the area. He needed to go down and assess the situation, but he was sure he'd be back in Edina by May.

Wilmath was impatient — she wanted to tell the man she loved that she now had a part of him — she had his son! It was a matter to be discussed in person.

In the meantime, there was more and more work to be done at the farm. Pete was continuing to go downhill, and Paulina and Wilmath, along with Vivian, Earl and Victor, had to do all the chores.

Seba Dennis came to the house one day the first part of May. He came to the door, saw Lottie and hoisted the little girl up into his big strong arms, giving her a hug and a kiss. Wilmath appeared at the door, and it was then that he saw a 10-month-old boy trying to stand and hold onto his mother's long skirt.

"You must be Bryan," he said, as he knelt and looked into the blue-green eyes of the little tot. Wilmath had written that she'd had a boy, but she'd never sent any pictures or described him. Looking at him now, he was taken aback — it was uncanny how much the boy resembled his own baby pictures! Well, maybe not — after all, it was his nephew!

"You're a good-looking guy," he said to the little lad. Wilmath wondered if he had noticed the resemblance, but she didn't utter a word.

After several moments of silence, she said, "I named him James Bryan, but we call him Jim."

They went into the house, where Paulina had already prepared lunch. Pete wanted to know what his son was doing down in Oklahoma.

"Well, Pa, there's lots of folks settlin' down there now," he told his father. "Quite a few Kansans are livin' in Cherokee, but down below the Cimarron River, there's a lot of southerners. Others have also been settlin' among the lands of the Five Civilized Tribes. Most of them are in the Choctaw and Chickasaw nations and in the southeast of the Creek and Cherokee nations. And you'd be surprised how many Germans have come to Oklahoma to homestead!"

Pete could tell that his son was very caught up in the swirl of the Oklahoma settling.

"Seba, do you think you might homestead down there?" asked Paulina.

"I think that's a very good possibility in the next couple of years," he answered. "I just gotta go when the time is right."

The conversation ended, and Pete went into the sitting room to lie down on the sofa. Seba remained in the kitchen with Paulina and Wilmath, who were clearing the dishes from the table. Seba looked into the sitting room where his dad was now sleeping peacefully. He looked at the family portrait on the wall and noticed that his father wasn't near as healthy as he had appeared in the picture, taken several years ago.

"Pete's not so well these days; he can't work any more," Paulina informed him.

Wilmath had put the children down for a nap upstairs and came down to the hallway, where she beckoned to Seba. "Let's take a walk down to the crick. We need to have that talk now." They started walking down to their "spot," and when they reached there, they sat down beside the old elm which still sported their initialed hearts.

"Seba, dear, I hardly know how to tell you this," she began. Seba had plucked some long blades of grass and was weaving them together in his hand, listening to her speak as he worked with his hands.

"Wilmath, you can always talk to me about anything," he said in a soft voice.

"Do you remember that night I spent with you in Edina when I was visiting Frank and Rosie?"

"How could I forget that — that would be like forgetting my own name. You know I have always had special feelings for you."

"Yes, and I have for you and always will have. But, now some things have changed!"

"How do you mean?"

"I am divorced now, and you and I have a bond between us that will be there forever. You see, my darling, Jim is your son! Can't you see yourself when you look at him?"

"Wilmath!! How can that be? You were still married to my brother before the child was born."

"Yes, I was, but remember — I wasn't living with him that fall night I spent with you in Edina, and when I went back to him two months later, I was already carrying your child. I only stayed with him a month after I went back to Love Lake, and he never stayed there with me the whole month — he was with Fannie!"

"Oh, my god, Wilmath — then, I am Jim's father — he's not John's!"

"That's right, dear — don't you see — I'm free now, and we have a child. We can be married!"

"Does John know he's mine?"

"No, he only knows that he's not his. He wanted to marry Fannie so bad that he agreed to let people think he's his son! He'd be a Dennis either way!"

"That's true — I have to say, this is quite a revelation!"

"Yes, and I can finally marry the man I should have married in the beginning. You and me have always had somethin' between us!"

"There's no denyin' that, Wilmath, but you know that I'm a wanderer and no tellin' where I'll end up! Besides, what would people say — what would our folks say — me marryin' my brother's wife?"

"What would we care — we love each other, Seba — and Jim needs a father. A boy needs a man around."

"That's true — but I can always be there for him as an uncle. I just don't want to create a scandal. You do understand, don't you, darling?"

Seba got up off the grassy bank and pulled Wilmath up so that she was standing beside him. She noticed that he had formed a perfect circle out of the woven grass. He placed the "grass ring" tenderly on the third finger of her left hand. Then he took her in his arms, kissed her on the lips — slowly — leaving her breathless!

He released her and looked into her eyes and said, "I will always love you, Wilmath — you are a real woman! You are strong, and I know that you will take good care of our son, and you will do what you need to for survival. There are few women with your grit and determination. I will keep in touch with you, and if you need to talk with me, I will always be there for you. We must think of our family. Pa is not going to be with us much longer. Paulina will be needin' your help — she still has young children to raise. We can't burden our folks with our problems now. I will be going back to Oklahoma — I'm not certain when. I may settle there. You belong here with the family."

Wilmath nodded her head affirmatively, telling herself that what he had said made sense. She reached up and planted a kiss quickly on his lips; then they started up toward the house.

Long after Seba had gone that day, Wilmath went to her room. She still had the grass ring in her pocket that he'd made earlier that day down by the crick. Before anything happened to it, she had better put it safely away. She got out the Bible that Martha Penrod had given her when she lived at Love Lake and pressed the woven circle of grass deeply into a seam between two of the pages. She had a feeling somehow that this might be the only ring she'd ever receive from Seba Dennis!

In the summer of 1899, Pete was barely able to get out of bed. Charley, Ren and John came down to put up the hay on their father's property. Wilmath and Paulina were busy caring for Pete, as well as the young children of the family. The Dennis brothers brought their friend, Harley Reardon, with them to help with the work. Vic and Earl, who were 13 and 12 respectively, were fast becoming hay hands that summer. Vivian was cooking for the crew, as well as for the family.

Wilmath said little to John, who was married to Fannie. It was an awkward situation, since he was still her stepbrother. Fannie had given birth to an infant several months after Wilmath had Jim. The boy lived only three days and died. There was a brief burial in the cemetery at Love Lake.

The fall crops were harvested by the brothers. Several neighbors and friends of Pete and Paulina's also helped. Harley Reardon had already gone down to Shelby County to Cherry Box, where he was building a new house for Frank and Rosie Thorn.

December 7, 1899, Simon Peter Dennis passed away. He had been bed-ridden for some time and suffered from dropsy. He was almost 67 years old! The funeral was held at the Dennis house. All of the Dennis children of the first and second family and the grandchildren were in attendance. Reverend Henderson came to the house from La Plata and officiated at the service.

Then, the family prepared to make the trip to the La Plata Cemetery, contending with a raw December wind. They had loaded Pete's body onto his wagon. Charley Dennis was designated to drive the team, with John sitting next to him. The horses' heads were veiled in black cloths, which were being whipped vigorously by the wind. Reverend Henderson followed in his buggy, with Ren accompanying him. Frank and Rosie Thorn, along with Seba, were lined up directly behind the buggy. Paulina and Wilmath and the other family members were in wagons behind them. The long cavalcade of conveyances drew much attention along the way, as they met other travelers on the road who pulled their rigs off to the side in quiet respect for their old neighbor and friend.

Once they reached the cemetery, Reverend Henderson recited a scripture, and old Pete's body was lowered to the ground to lie at rest next to the body of his little daughter, Orena. Then, after hugging Paulina tightly, the members of the first Dennis family went to their homes in Love Lake and Edina, bundling up well to protect themselves against the penetrating wind.

CHAPTER EIGHT

ON DECEMBER 31, Frank and Rosie Thorn had planned a housewarming and New Year's Eve party at their new home in Cherry Box. Invitations had been sent out before Pete's death, and Rosie had written Paulina immediately after the funeral, asking her if she thought they should cancel the party out of respect for her father. Paulina had written back, telling her that Pete would have wanted her to go ahead with the celebration. Rosie had also written to Wilmath, inviting her to come for this gala occasion, knowing that she needed to be around some young people. After all, she had been tied down on the farm, caring for Pete and helping her mother.

Wilmath hated to leave Ma with all the work and especially now, but Paulina told her daughter that she needed to consider accepting the Thorns' invitation. Wilmath finally decided that she would go. Rosie had said that Harley Reardon's cousin and his wife, Fred and Ada Milford who were living at Gibbs, had insisted that, should Wilmath decide to attend, they would be happy to stop by the Dennis farm and bring her to Cherry Box. They would arrive the day before the party, as Fred Milford wanted to inspect his cousin's latest carpenter work. They were also looking forward to the housewarming and New Year's Eve celebration.

Wilmath was glad the weather was halfway decent the next to the last day in December. The Milfords would be there early, as the ride to Cherry Box would take a good part of the day. She had a small bag packed and was waiting for them, when she noticed a buggy coming up the lane. She bid the family a hasty good-bye and hurried out the door, so that the couple wouldn't be further detained.

Ada and Fred Milford greeted her, and Wilmath settled down in the buggy's back seat. Ada handed her a quilt, in case she got a chill.

The Milfords had lived on a farm east of the Dennis' until a few months ago, when they moved to the town of Gibbs. Business there was booming, and Fred Milford had opened a feed store and livery stable. In fact, there were two other feed stores and livery stables in Gibbs. There was a hotel, a bank, a grocery store and the Square Deal Store, which was a dry goods store. Two doctors practiced there.

Harley Reardon had made his home with his cousin since his parents, Miranda and Joshua, had moved to Ozark County, near Theodosia, Missouri. Miranda had been the first child born to Oscar and Elizabeth Milford, who had lived about two miles east of the Dennis farm. Oscar had died in 1885, leaving each of his children well off. Harley Reardon wanted to remain near the families of both of his parents. When he wasn't building houses, gates or doing carpentry work, the young man helped area farmers. Sometimes he helped his cousin, Fred, at the feed store and livery stable.

Fred Milford was less than average in height. None of his family was tall. His wife was small and petite, too. Wilmath noticed that Ada was dressed in the latest fashions, and she was fascinated with the large hat adorning her head! She'd never seen such fancy hat!

"Ada, I just have to tell you how grand your hat is!" Wilmath exclaimed.

"Oh, thank you, Wilmath," she said politely. "I bought this from Hattie Young at the hat shop in the front area of the post office at Gibbs when the new fall shipment came in."

Wilmath knew that Ada was a talker. Fred sat quietly up front, interjecting a word or two occasionally into the conversations. Ada told her that Fred and several of the other trustees of the Methodist Church were trying to see about getting a new church building built at Gibbs. They were temporarily holding services upstairs over the bank building. Wilmath knew the Milfords were staunch churchgoers.

She had almost been lulled to sleep by Ada's endless prattle when she heard her mention Seba's name. Wide awake now, Wilmath asked, "What, Ada?" What did you just say about Seba?"

"Well, I was just saying that one of your relatives is marrying one of ours — Seba Dennis is marrying Fred's cousin, Nora Wilks."

"Surely you must be mistaken, Ada. I've heard nothing of it!"

"Well, Nora's been staying in Edina off and on with one of her aunts, who lives next door to Seba. In fact, they're getting married in two weeks at our Methodist Church at Gibbs!"

"She's right, Wilmath. We're invited to the wedding," Fred added in support of his wife's announcement. Wilmath nearly fell out of the buggy in shock! Ada's words astounded her! She suddenly felt like her heart was as chilled as her two feet that were now protruding out from under the quilt that Wilmath had covered up with only minutes ago!

Ada was talking about something else by now, but Wilmath wasn't listening much. They had turned south onto the road that would take them through the town of Cherry Box. Wilmath tried to make idle talk, mostly in answer to Ada's questions, but the news that had come from Ada's lips concerning Seba's upcoming marriage had blocked almost everything else out of her mind.

It was late afternoon when they arrived at Cherry Box. They had to go another mile west of the town to reach the Thorns' new farmhouse. The sun was going down when they turned up a long lane, lined with rows of cedar trees on each side. A new two-story house appeared, smoke curling out profusely from its two chimneys, as they rode farther down the lane. Soon they pulled up to the house where Frank Thorn and Harley Reardon were waiting to help the ladies alight.

Inside the house, Rosie was waiting to give each lady a hug, then insisted they have a seat near the fireplace in the parlor where a fire was burning brightly.

"Poor dears," she sympathized, "you must be hungry as well as cold. I have supper prepared — the men will be in soon from stabling the horse in the barn, and then we'll eat." Wilmath looked around while they awaited the meal. She envied Rosie — having the latest furnishings available at that time and everything so new and clean! She knew that Frank and Rosie had worked hard for what they had. Some day she'd have a nice clean home, too!

The men were coming in through the side porch, taking off coats and gloves and hanging them on the hangers on a wall in the hallway that led to the kitchen.

"My goodness, Rosie, you've certainly prepared enough food for a thrashing crew!" Ada exclaimed. All of them sat down at the table. Too soon, talk turned to family news.

"I guess you all know we'll almost be related, once my brother marries your cousin Nora," Rosie told the Milfords.

"Oh, that's right — I'm sure that you all are invited to the wedding," Ada answered.

"No, Ada — Seba told us that Nora thought it would be poor taste for us to go to the church, attendin' a public occasion, with Pa dyin' so recently. He's only asked our mother and Grandma Reid to the wedding," Rosie explained to her guest. "I gather that he really just wanted a quiet ceremony before a justice of the peace, but Nora wanted it to be at the church."

Wilmath sat quietly, listening to the talk of Seba's wedding plans. Finally, thinking that she should somehow make an attempt at some conversation, she asked, "How is Grandma Reid doing?"

"She just had her 83rd birthday, Willie, and guess what — she's going to move down here in the old house on the other side of our property some time this year. Mother has been listenin' to Seba talk about goin' to Oklahoma to settle on some of that free land, and Grandma's afraid that Mother'll want to settle down there, too. Then, she'd be left at Love Lake all alone. Charley, John and Ren are thinkin' about goin' to Oklahoma, too."

Wilmath knew that Rosie had always been close to Phoebe Reid. She'd even been named for her grandmother, being Martha's only daughter. Wilmath had always liked Grandma Reid and had thought of her as a "good old soul." She would be lucky to have Rosie to look after her.

After the evening meal Wilmath asked to be excused and headed upstairs to the bedroom that Rosie had prepared for her. She had a terrible headache and quickly got ready for bed. She heard the others come upstairs — the Thorns going to their room to the east of hers and the Milfords going to the west bedroom. Harley Reardon had been staying in one end of the smokehouse that had served as his living quarters while he'd been here building the Thorns' house. Wilmath decided he was probably still sleeping out there. He was four years older than Wilmath — of average height — a bit taller than his cousin Fred, and had light brown hair and a thin mustache. The slender young man seemed outgoing and friendly.

Wilmath's thoughts turned once more to the news of Seba's upcoming marriage to Nora. She knew little about the girl except that she was related to the Milfords and had always seemed devoutly religious. She finally drifted off to sleep after lying awake for some time, unable to rid her mind of the heartbreaking news!

CHAPTER NINE

NEW YEAR'S EVE was a sunny but chilly day in Shelby County. The Thorn house was bustling with activity as things were being put in order for the housewarming celebration and dance. Rosie had made several pies, and Ada had brought several cakes. The men were busy rolling up the new carpets for the dance that would take place that night.

Neighbors and friends of the Thorns poured into the house that evening to celebrate and welcome in the new year. Frank had his fiddle out — tuning the strings to reflect perfect melodious tones. Rosie was seated at the pump organ — one of the few pieces of furniture she'd saved from their old house. Soon strains of "Camptown Races" and "There is a Tavern in the Town" could be heard coming harmoniously from their instruments. The dancing started, led by the Milfords.

Wilmath felt someone tugging at the sleeve of her dress, asking her to dance — it was Harley Reardon. "What do you say, Wilmath, shall we 'cut a rug' for these folks and show them how it's done?"

She hesitated, and then thought, Why not? Aloud, she said, "Let's." They made a picturesque scene on the dance floor.

"Why, Mr. Reardon, you are quite good," she complimented him.

"Not bad on your part either, Wilmath," he answered kindly. Before she realized it, she had danced almost every dance with Harley.

After the pies and cakes had been cut and devoured, the crowd commenced dancing again, eagerly awaiting the new year of 1900 — the turn of a new century! Wilmath suddenly felt herself biting back tears for some reason! Harley noticed, and before she knew it he was leading her out through the kitchen and through the side porch door into the cool night air.

"Come on, Wilmath — maybe we need some fresh air," he suggested.

"No, Harley, really — I'll be fine. I think I may be a bit too tired to dance any more."

"Well, then, why don't we go over to my little shack where it's warm and we'll talk?" He led her out beyond the yard where the smokehouse stood. She waited while he opened the door, and as soon as they were in out of the cold, he lit a lantern. The room was tiny — only a cot for a bed, a small table and a straight-backed chair. A wood-burning stove sat in one corner of the room. Since there was only one chair, he offered it to Wilmath, while he sat on the side of the cot.

"Now, Wilmath, are you feeling a bit better?" he asked considerately.

"Yes, I guess I am just thinking about Pa dying and Ma beginning the new year without him."

Harley Reardon couldn't help noticing the sad blue eyes of this beautiful woman. He walked slowly over to the chair, putting both of his arms around her. She realized that it felt good once more to be held. Harley put his lips on her cheek — smelling the sweet smell of lilacs as he got closer to her. Then, turning her to face him, he kissed her on lush, half-open lips. He extended his hand to her in a quiet gesture, and led her over to the cot, where they sank gently down, he covering her ripe body with his. She seemed not to care about much else except the warmth of his body and the ardent kisses he was now planting on her lips. She returned his caresses and kisses, desire welling up deep inside her. His desires were intensifying also. Both then strived to satisfy this shared feeling, and soon their efforts were rewarded. The emptiness that the news of the day before had brought on had temporarily been filled for her, while his needs that had gone unattended for some time had been met.

It was almost midnight as the couple made their way back into the noisy house. People were lauding in the new year with toasts and new resolutions. Wilmath made her own private resolution — she'd show Seba Dennis — he, Oklahoma and his soon-to-be bride could simply drop off the ends of the earth as far as she was concerned. Harley made his way to her, handing her a glass of punch. She raised it up and proposed a toast, "Here's to 1900 — and new beginnings!"

The day after the party, Harley Reardon rode home with Wilmath and the Milfords. The cold January wind started to rear up. By the time they reached La Plata, bidding Wilmath farewell at the Dennis', snow had started to fall and was increasing steadily as they continued on to Gibbs.

Harley had promised Wilmath that he would be calling on her soon, and he kept his word. He and Wilmath went to parties and had become frequent guests of Harley's cousin, Ollie and her husband, Joe Saunders in Macon. Ollie was a year younger than Wilmath, and the Saunders' had just been married a year. The two ladies seemed to gravitate toward each other instantly, becoming good friends. Wilmath found that Ollie was easy to talk to, and the women shared many confidences while the men talked of farming and building.

Ollie had been embroiled in a tragic situation after Wilmath had given birth to Lottie in 1896. Ollie's mother, Lucinda (Reardon), had been married to Thomas Vanderpool. They were the parents of four children; Ollie was the eldest. When Ollie was 12, her mother died of tuberculosis. Her father, a small man, had been terribly sorrowed by his young wife's death. Two years later, he had married a lady named Beulah. They soon began quarreling, and Thomas could see the marriage wasn't going to last. The Vanderpool children spent most of the time living with their grandmother, Ursula Reardon, in Macon.

One evening Thomas and Beulah had an argument of mammoth proportions. It had escalated to the point that Thomas had grown despondent, had seized a knife and stabbed Buelah. He had quite a chore on his hands, as she was a large woman. After she had ceased breathing, Thomas had started stabbing himself with the knife. Then he had passed out, and when he came to, several men were standing over him, while others were hauling Beulah's dead body out of the house.

Ollie had come home from her grandmother's house, and upon entering the house had seen her dead stepmother on the floor — her father lying there wounded. The girl left the house, screaming at the top of her lungs, running all the way to the closest neighbor's house for help.

Thomas Vanderpool was put in the Macon County jail and

wouldn't defend himself or allow any legal defense. The judge had no choice but to sentence him to die by hanging on November 13, 1896. The hanging was to take place in the courtyard north of the old jail. The sheriff issued tickets to a small crowd that was there to witness the execution. Several thousand people were in Macon that day. After Vanderpool's body was taken to a local funeral parlor, the crowd filed by to take a last look at him.

Poor Ollie! Her life had already been fraught with so much pain, and she was barely 18 years old! The two women vowed to be friends forever — after all, they'd probably be related one of these days!

By April, Wilmath and Harley had been courting for three months. I could do worse than Harley, she thought — he's related to the Milfords, and I might as well be one as Seba. She'd heard little about the wedding, except that the newlyweds were living at Edina and were soon preparing to go to Oklahoma.

One day Wilmath told Paulina that it was likely that she'd soon be Mrs. Harley Reardon.

"Hmmmph!" Paulina grunted, "I wouldn't count on that! Harley's mother, Miranda, is quite a possessive and difficult woman. She's always acted uppity."

"Well, Ma, she's not even livin' around here. I doubt she'd be a problem." Wilmath soon discovered that she was the one with a problem! She hadn't given too much thought to the fact that she was gaining weight — she was getting a little older — look at Ma. Still, she realized she hadn't been feeling quite normal lately.

Not wanting to alert Ma to the situation needlessly, she went to see Dr. Thompson. She hadn't seen him since she'd had that spell of pneumonia when she'd lived at Love Lake. He had moved his practice from Atlanta to La Plata now that old Doctor Gates had retired and had sold his office to the new doctor. After a brief examination, Dr. Thompson told Wilmath that she was indeed pregnant!

The pregnancy weighed heavily on her mind! Harley had that job working at the feed store and livery stable in Gibbs when he wasn't carpentering. At least they'd have a good living!

The following weekend, Harley came by, and the couple went to La Plata for the annual May Day celebration. A maypole had been set up on the little square in the middle of town, ready for the young people to do the maypole dance. Joe and Ollie Saunders met them there, and the couples had a fun-filled day, participating in the festivities. On the way home, Wilmath asked Harley to stop the wagon by a shady clump of trees close to where an old house had once stood. There in the shade she revealed her startling news.

"Harley, we're going to have a baby. It'll most likely be in the fall, around October."

He was taken aback by the news and was speechless for a few moments! The fragrance of some spring flowers, growing randomly along a remnant of an old fence near where the old house had once stood scented the evening air.

When Harley had recovered and was able to speak, he replied, "Are you sure?"

"Yes," she nodded.

"This is a surprise! I had assumed you knew a few things — you havin' those two kids already." Wilmath said nothing.

"What will we do now?" he asked.

"I thought probably we'd get married — you know, Harley, I am a hard worker. I've done most of the chores since Pa died. I could be a lot of help to you."

"I wasn't plannin' to get married quite this soon," he stated honestly.

"Well, I think we should go ahead and marry as soon as possible before I get any farther along."

Harley admitted, "This just has been a shock! I'll have to tell my folks!" Wilmath could see that the discussion was temporarily at an end, due to the silence that followed. Soon Harley was calling a swift "giddiyap" to the horse, and down the road they went.

When they reached the Dennis' house, Harley stopped, gave her a quick kiss on the cheek and said, "I'll have to go down to Theodosia and explain this to Ma and Pa. Then we'll figure out our plans." Wilmath only nodded and climbed down from the wagon. She waved to Harley — an odd chill coming over her for some reason!

Several weeks went by, and Wilmath heard nothing from Harley. Summing up all the courage she had, she took the Santa Fe to Gibbs to Fred Milford's feed store. Fred saw her coming, and knowing they would need to speak privately, he greeted her and then guided her to a room in back of the store. She noticed the place was full of bulging sacks of grain and corn. He brought two chairs back and sat near the door to make sure he didn't miss any of the customers' business. Luckily, it was close to the noon hour, so trade would be slim for awhile.

"I guess you know why I've come," Wilmath began, sadness enveloping her blue eyes.

"Yes, I can imagine, Wilmath," he confessed.

"I've heard nothing from Harley since the night I told him I was havin' his baby in the fall. Where is he anyway?"

"This is a very difficult thing to have to tell you, dear, but you are entitled to know the truth. Harley is down in Ozark County at Theodosia with Aunt Miranda. He's not coming back up here — they want him to stay down there. He went to talk to his folks about your problem, and his mother got very 'worked up.' She told Harley that if he even thought of marrying you and claiming the 'bastard' child, he'd never get a cent of his inheritance. She further told him she felt like you were a very 'loose' woman, and she'd not have her son marrying beneath him!"

Tears formed at the rims of Wilmath's eyes upon hearing the cruel words of Harley's mother. Soon a stream of tears cascaded down her face, and her shoulders started to shake as her sobbing continued.

Fred Milford stood and placed his arm around her shoulder. "Wilmath, I'm so sorry," he said softly. "My aunt has always been temperamental, and she's always been 'high and mighty' in attitude. She'd be a formidable enemy as a mother-in-law!"

Drying her eyes on a handkerchief he had just handed her, she gathered her wits and replied, "Some day Harley will have to stand up to his mother if he wishes to have a life of his own. I suppose she has hoped to save him from this disgrace by insisting that he stay down there. She figures that Theodosia, being so close to Arkansas, will be far enough away that he won't be near me when I have this baby. Well, I have news for them — there are plenty of Milfords around Gibbs, and I am going to give this baby the last name of Reardon. Some of them will have to face this!"

"I certainly have to admire your spunk, but I doubt if giving the baby the Reardon name will change anything. I'm going to have to wait on a customer who is just coming in — do you want to wait here and collect your thoughts a moment?"

"No, Fred, I think I'll go out the back — I have to get back to La Plata to decide how to continue on with my life." She gathered the small amount of dignity she had left, stood up tall and straight and started out the back door of the feed store.

"Wilmath, I'm sorry," he said again as he started for the front of the store. She had already hurried out the door, thus his words fell on deaf ears.

When she arrived at Ma's house, she related the conversation to Paulina, who sat with her broad chunky arms folded tightly. When she'd finished her account of her visit to Gibbs, Paulina said nothing, with a resigned look on her face.

"Ma, what do you think I should do?"

"Nothin' you can do — I already knew that Reardon woman wouldn't go along with this. She's always been high-strung and saucy. None of the other kids of Oscar and Elizabeth Milford are like that! I think she was just spoiled and self-centered — bein' the first born and all. You better just make your peace with this — she'll never let that boy marry you!"

Paulina proved to be right about the situation. As the leaves began to fall in rural La Plata, Wilmath still had received no word from Harley. His cousin, Ollie, had remained her faithful friend, and she and Joe had come to visit once or twice since Harley had left. Ollie told Wilmath that she could consider them lifetime friends.

She knew the baby was about to be born when, during the first week of October, she'd started experiencing some pain. By the eighth, she told Paulina to summon Samantha Jenkins. The pain was very severe! Samantha had only run up the stairs, taken one look at Wilmath, and knew this one was not going to be an easy birth. Paulina had Earl saddle up old Dolly and ride into La Plata to get Dr. Thompson.

It seemed like Earl had been gone for hours to Paulina, who was getting more worried by the minute. Soon he arrived, with Dr. Thompson in his buggy directly behind him. The doctor made his way into the house, bounded up the stairs and saw that Wilmath was almost unconscious from the pain. Samantha had told him immediately that the baby was a "feet first" and that the young mother was worn out from all the straining and pushing.

Dr. Thompson worked diligently and gently. It was awhile before those waiting downstairs heard the lusty cry of the new-born baby. Paulina was relieved — she thought the child might not make it! She had remained downstairs with Lottie and Jim.

Finally the doctor came downstairs, a tired and weary look on his face. "Well, folks," he said, "you have a little girl." Then he took Paulina aside and said, "Wilmath's had a rough time having this child. I had to perform a little surgery. She'll be okay in a few days. I've given her some laudanum, and she'll sleep for the rest of the day. One thing, though — she'll never be able to have more children!" After adding that somber note, the doctor left.

Late that evening, Wilmath woke up and looked at the sleeping baby that lay in the bed beside her. Paulina was sitting beside the bed, looking at mother and child.

"Well, dear, it looks like you had another little girl," she smiled.

Wilmath was groggy from the medicine, but she said weakly, "She will be named Ollie Ellen Reardon — after my best friend, Ollie Saunders and Aunt Ellen. I decided that a few weeks ago, if it was a girl."

Paulina sadly informed her, "Dr. Thompson had to do some surgery during the birth. He said that you can never have any more children."

Wilmath remained silent, but she thought, that's quite all right with me — I'll not have a house full of kids!

Aloud, she said, "Little Ollie is plump and healthy. That's all that matters, Ma."

Paulina left the room, hoping that Wilmath could get some rest and get her strength back. After the door closed, Wilmath looked over at her sleeping little daughter.

"Well, Ollie," she whispered, "you will be named Reardon whether they like it or not!"

Paulina needn't have worried about Wilmath regaining her strength — October 8, 1900, was a turning point for a strengthening process that would begin inside the 19-year-old woman. That strength would be tested over and over throughout the rest of her life!

CHAPTER TEN

BY THE MIDDLE OF OCTOBER 1900, Seba Dennis and his new wife, Nora, had been in Oklahoma Territory for four months. Seba had to admire Nora — she was a tiny thing — barely over five feet tall; yet she possessed a lot of spunk, fire and determination. Her auburn hair and sparkling brown eyes attested to these qualities. Her personality, particularly these traits, reminded Seba of Wilmath.

The couple had heard all kinds of stories as soon as they neared the northern Oklahoma border. They passed wagons with signs reading "Bald-knobbed in Mizzouri" and "Oklihonny or bust." These people were looking forward to starting a brand new society or else restarting their lives in a new area.

Kansans were the main settlers in northern Oklahoma Territory, and most Missourians were settling in the upper Cherokee section. Rumors along the way indicated that the government planned to open up lands in the southwest corner of the territory in 1901. This land supposedly contained gold and silver, and, possibly buried Spanish Treasure. Instead of having the runs, as in the past, the government was considering holding a lottery, giving equal chances to spectators and homesteaders.

Seba and Nora made their way to the small northwestern area near Woodward. There they stayed in a hotel until they could decide where they wanted to settle. Nora hated the town! It was a wild, disorderly place — 23 saloons were already in business here. The sale of intoxicating beverages was legal, but the Indians were prohibited from buying spirits. Saloons were linked to brawling, crime and prostitution. Some of the establishments dispensed drinks from fancy mahogany bars. Risqué portraits hung from the walls, and there were female card dealers. Nora had never seen the like!

One of the first things she wanted to do when they got settled was to join the local Methodist Church. The number of churches paled greatly beside the number of saloons. Once a member, she became active in the Women's Christian Temperance Union. Carrie Nation had been to Guthrie which was southeast of Woodward, where Seba and Nora had attended a meeting concerning prohibition. Pamphlets were handed out, and Nora came back to Woodward, eager to pass them out around the corrupt town!

"I'd be mighty careful about handin' out those things around the saloons — you might get accosted by those drunks that hang around there," he warned his wife.

"If everyone felt that way, nobody would get laws passed and this awful behavior would just go on and on," she insisted.

Seba was searching for a place to build a home. He wanted to start farming the new land. The area around Woodward was just right, and it was available. Nora thought they should wait awhile before they decided on a permanent location.

January 1901, the couple moved to a small log house several miles southeast of Woodward. A farmer there had been called back to Kansas due to the grave illness of a family member, and Nora and Seba rented the farm during his absence.

Nora spent most of her time at the church and at the temperance meetings in Woodward. Seba had the use of the farmer's team and wagon to cut wood, as the landowner had taken the train to Kansas. There were two extra horses on the property, and many mornings after breakfast Nora would ask Seba to saddle one of the horses so that she could ride into town.

One day close to the first of February she had gone to the temperance meeting in town. The speaker had fired all the ladies up, and they had decided to march over to some of the saloons, forming a line just outside the swinging doors. They began to sing hymns and to also pass out prohibition literature. Hearing the commotion outside, the men came out to see what was going on. Most went back inside and ignored the band of ladies. Some of them, however, were angered by the interfering women. Two men at one of the saloons had watched the women intently off and on as they marched up to first one of the establishments and then the other.

It was nearing the end of the day, and the ladies, tired from their endeavor, decided to depart for their homes. Nora went to the stable to fetch her horse. She climbed up in the saddle, aided by the livery owner, and headed homeward.

Seba began to worry — it was almost dark and there was no sign of Nora. He decided to saddle the other horse and ride into town. She was always home by this time of day! Before he got halfway to town, he saw her horse standing by a walnut tree along the road. When he got closer, he saw a small crumpled form lying near the trunk of the tree.

"Nora, oh, Nora, what in the world!" he cried as he got off the horse and ran toward his wife's body. He saw that she had been badly beaten, then strangled to death! Her body was still warm — it had happened just recently! He would have to lift her still body and lay it over her horse and get her the rest of the way to town.

When he got into Woodward, he went to the town's only funeral parlor. Still unable to believe that this awful incident had just occurred, he then went to the sheriff's office.

"Sheriff, I just found my wife beaten and strangled out on the road toward the place we're stayin' at. I want you to find the murderer or murderers, whichever the case may be."

"Well, Mr. Dennis, you know it's tough tryin' to keep things peaceful in this town right now. Where was your wife headin' when this crime occurred?"

"She had been in town all day at the church or maybe a temperance meeting. She was headin' home — she was always back before dark. I don't know who would have wanted to kill Nora!"

The sheriff could see that this man was experiencing shock and disbelief at the death of his young wife.

"I'll go out there tomorrow when it's daylight and take a look around the area where you found your wife. That's about all I can do for now."

Seba went back to the undertaker's establishment to make arrangements to take Nora back to Missouri. He would ride back on the train with her poor little maimed body!

The next morning, getting very little sleep the night before, Seba went into Woodward to the sheriff's office. The deputy on duty told him that the sheriff would be back shortly — he'd gone to some of the saloons to check out a few things. Soon the sheriff returned.

"Mr. Dennis, I rode out to that walnut tree this morning. Did you stop there and look around?"

"No, sir, I just couldn't. I was pretty upset and I didn't know what to look for anyway."

"I went down into the woods a ways beyond that tree, and I found a couple of empty whiskey bottles. I also saw two different sets of footprints, which means that there were probably two of them. Was your wife one of them temperance ladies?"

"Yes, my wife definitely believed drinking should be outlawed!"

"That is pretty much what I thought — I do know that those ladies were over in front of several of the saloons yesterday, pretty fired up about this temperance thing — singin' and passin' out some pamphlets. It's most likely a couple of those drunks followed her home and killed her. I went to the saloons, asking questions, and all of them said they didn't see a thing or know anything about it. It's gonna be mighty hard tryin' to find the murderers — probably impossible! I'm sorry for you. Is there anything I can do to help you with the arrangements or burial?"

"No, sir, thank you, but I need to go to the telegraph office and then have the undertaker load her body onto the train — I'm takin' her back to Missouri for burial."

Seba had sent a telegram to Nora's parents, Fern and Homer Wilks, in Adair County. He was riding the Santa Fe on past Gibbs to the next town, which was Brashear. He would be met at the depot by Foster Easley, who ran an undertaking business in the town. The Wilks' would travel to Brashear, where Seba would meet with them to discuss the arrangements.

Foster Easley was a close family friend of the Wilks'. Recently, he had gotten his license as an embalmer and opened his funeral establishment. He was also a member of the Brashear Methodist Church. It was here that Seba and his in-laws had decided to hold the funeral. Nora would have wanted the funeral held at a church, and in Gibbs the Methodist Church was still meeting up over the bank. A church building would be necessary, as there were many relatives and friends.

Seba's family as well had been notified. Martha Penrod, Charley Dennis and family, Ren and Mollie, and John and Fannie were coming for the funeral from Love Lake. Frank and Rosie Thorn were driving up from Cherry Box.

The church was full the day of the funeral! As expected, most of the Milford family was there. Four sons of Oscar and Elizabeth Milford and their families were present. Ollie and Joe Saunders were present, as well as Fred and Ada Milford. Several of the Wilks' family and friends had attended.

The burial was to be in the Milford Cemetery, which was located on a three-acre tract on the farm of Oscar Milfred, now owned by their son, Raymond. After the funeral, the procession made its way south to Gibbs, going through the town and turning west and on down a dirt road that would take them to the cemetery on the east side of the road. A wrought-iron fence enclosed the graveyard. Buried there already were the Milford parents and several of their children who had died in infancy. There were a few graves of other Milford relatives, as well as some of the Wilks'.

Fred Milford read some scripture out of the Bible, and Raymond Milford ended the brief service with a prayer. Then Nora's body was laid to rest in the freshly dug earth. Seba and Nora had only been married one year!

Frank and Rosie Thorn took Seba aside — they wondered where the bereaved man would be going now — or if he even had a place to stay.

"Seba, if you don't have any plans right now, we'd like you to come to Cherry Box with us and live. You could stay with us, or you could go over and stay at Grandma Reid's," offered Rosie.

"I could use your help on the farm for a while, too," Frank added.

"I just don't think I can go back to Oklahoma right now, but I will probably go back in a year or so and homestead somewhere around Woodward. I'm going to write to the sheriff and see if they have been able to find out who killed Nora." After thinking a moment about the Thorn's kind offer, he said, "Yes, I'll go home with you two to Cherry Box."

Before he left, he shook hands with relatives and friends. The Thorns were waiting, and he was just getting ready to start toward their buggy when he was detained by Andrew Milford's widow, Cecilia, and her two daughters, Annette and Lila.

"Seba," Cecilia said kindly, "my daughters and I live near Leonard. I couldn't help overhearing you talk with the Thorns about going to live at Cherry Box. I just wanted to say that if you get over to Leonard, look us up — I'd like to have you take a meal with us sometime."

"Thank you, Cecilia. I had forgotten that you had moved down there. I'll be sure to do that when I'm in the area." Seba noticed that the oldest daughter, Annette, was about his age. She was a pretty girl with black hair and brown eyes — slender and approximately five foot five inches tall. Annette resembled her mother's side of the family, the Sloans — she looked nothing like the Milfords.

Seba said good-bye to the Milford ladies and got into the Thorns' buggy. The weather that day had been unseasonably warm — almost 60 degrees. He knew the middle of February in this part of the country could be cold and snowy. He supposed the temperature was something to be thankful for, if one could feel that way at all just after losing a young wife whose fate had been in the hands of two murderous drunks!

On the way to Cherry Box, the Thorns had thought of stopping at Paulina's, but then decided it might not be best right now, with Wilmath having a new baby whose father was related to the Milfords. Besides, they needed to get home before too late, and it was quite a distance to the farm. On they drove, arriving at Cherry Box while it was still daylight.

CHAPTER ELEVEN

IF THEY HAD STOPPED by the Dennis place on the way home from the burial, they would have been aware of some of the changes that had taken place three months earlier at the farm.

When Ollie was almost a month old, a new family had moved into the neighborhood. John Sidner, an 87-year-old pensioner, and his wife, Mary, who was in her mid-40s, had rented a house a mile north of the Dennis'. Paulina and Wilmath had taken an apple pie to their new neighbors' house to welcome them to the community. The Sidners had a son, Lewis, who was four years old.

Mary Sidner pleasantly invited the ladies into the house and thanked them for the pie. She told them that her husband spent most of his time in bed. They had lived in Quincy but had decided to come to Adair County to be near her brother, John Greer. While they were visiting, the back door opened, and a tall man with jet- black hair appeared. He was extremely handsome, and Wilmath thought he might be about 30. In a moment or two, he came into the sitting room.

"David, I want you to meet our neighbors, Paulina and Wilmath Dennis," Mary said to her son.

"I'm pleased to meet you both," David smiled, revealing gleaming white teeth. Wilmath thought he was one of the best-looking fellows she'd ever seen!

"We're happy to meet you, Mr. Sidner," Wilmath mumbled.

David corrected her, "My name is Blackburn — John is my stepfather. I keep this place goin' since Ma needs someone here who can do the work."

"I just don't know what we'd do without David," Mary said gratefully. Paulina was getting ready to go back home — they had the evening chores to do yet. Earl was becoming a good helper, but it was like pulling hens' teeth to get Vic to do anything.

As Wilmath followed her mother toward the door, David approached Wilmath. "Miss Dennis, may I come to call on you?" Wilmath was surprised by his boldness.

"Well, David — I am divorced and I have three children. We all live with Ma and my brothers and sisters."

"All right, then," he corrected himself quickly, "Mrs. Dennis, may I come to call on you?" Wilmath didn't know what to say. She thought about his request for a minute.

"It's okay by me, David — do you know where we live?"

"Yes, I think I do! And, I shall be coming by very soon!" The two Dennis women left, with Wilmath filled with awe at the sudden actions on the part of this young neighbor.

Two days later David Blackburn arrived at the Dennis household and asked Wilmath to go to a dance with him at La Plata. The holidays were arriving quickly — it would soon be Thanksgiving and then Christmas. David became a frequent guest of the Dennis family.

It was only a few weeks before David approached the subject of marriage.

"Wilmath, you know, I'm 33, and I'd like to settle down and have a place of my own. Of course, I'd have to live close enough to Ma to be able to help them every day, too. You're a mighty fine-lookin' woman, and I'd be proud to have you for my wife!"

"David, there is something I have to tell you — I'm unable to bear any more children. I don't know if that matters to you or not. Also, my three children will have to live with us."

"I never thought much about children of my own — your three will be there, so that will be plenty. What about getting married the first of January?"

"That's pretty sudden, isn't it? We've only known each other a few weeks!"

"I don't think these things can be measured in time, dear. I really do want you for my wife," he insisted.

Wilmath knew she wasn't in love with David Blackburn. But she had lived there with Ma quite a while, and the relief of having four less mouths to feed might help Ma. Besides, any woman would be lucky to have such an attractive husband!

Christmas 1900 went by swiftly, as Wilmath's marriage to

David was being planned. He had rented a small farm halfway between the Sidners' and Paulina's. That way, Wilmath could be close to her family as well. She had written her friend, Ollie Saunders, and she and Joe wrote back and said they'd be glad to come up to La Plata and be present at the ceremony.

January 7, 1901, Wilmath and David went to La Plata to obtain a marriage license. Although there was no snow on the ground, it was bitterly cold in Macon County. The Saunders' were coming up from Macon on the Wabash that day. David and Wilmath waited at the depot after going to get the license, and at three o'clock that afternoon the train came into view from the south, carrying their friends as passengers. Ollie was happy to see Wilmath. Joe and David went to the livery and shortly returned with the team and wagon. Several heavy quilts were distributed to keep everyone as warm as possible, and then they were heading toward the Dennis farm.

Ollie, who was sitting in back with Wilmath, whispered to her friend, "Oh, Willie, he's so good-looking — where in the world did you find such a catch?"

"The truth is, Ollie, he 'caught' me," she laughed quietly.

The two women talked excitedly on the way to the farm, and Ollie indicated she was eager to see her little namesake, who was only three months old. When they got to the house, David and Joe helped the ladies out; then Joe carried in a small valise containing enough clothes for him and his wife for two days.

Paulina got the Saunders' settled in, and David went on down the road to his farm and also to his folks' before dark to do their chores. He and Earl talked briefly, agreeing that they would need to take two wagons to La Plata the next day. Besides the bride and groom, there would be the Saunders', Paulina, Earl and Mary Sidner and her son, Lewis. Vivian and Vic were staying home with the younger Dennis children.

January 8, 1901, was a cold bleak day. The temperature was hovering near 20 degrees. At 10 a.m., Earl had the team and wagon ready to go, and David turned into the lane shortly thereafter. The wedding party departed from the house on the way to La Plata where the justice of the peace would marry Wilmath and David. H.D. Bunch performed the brief ceremony at 11 a.m.

Snow had started to fall, and it looked like Macon County would soon be blanketed with several inches or even several feet of snow. Ollie and John decided to get on the train while in town and travel back to Macon in lieu of the bad weather. They hugged Wilmath, wished the young married couple well, and then went inside the depot to wait for the train.

The dirt roads were white with snow and filling up fast, as the Blackburns and Earl made their way northeast to Paulina's. Wilmath went into the house just long enough to bundle up little Ollie, whom she was still nursing, and took her quickly outside and climbed in the wagon with David, Mary and Lewis. Paulina had decided beforehand that Lottie and Jim should stay with them a few days and give the young couple a chance to get settled in their new home. The snow came steadily down, and it would be a week before the roads could be traveled again!

Lottie, age 5, and Jim, age 3, were getting settled in their new home. Jim liked playing with David's little brother, Lewis, as they were close to the same age. Mary Sidner was a good grandmother to all of the kids, but she had little time to spend with them or Lewis, due to the ill health of her husband.

As time went on, it appeared that David was jealous of the three children because he thought they demanded a lot of attention. Little Ollie needed to be near her mother most of all, and that proved to be a sore spot with David.

"That baby always needs you," he'd complain, "and she's always cryin'."

"Of course, she does, David — she's only a few months old," Wilmath countered.

Wilmath had a garden, and she was teaching Lottie and Jim to help her tend it and harvest the vegetables. She had a few chickens, which she kept in an old dilapidated chicken house on the property, and the two children gathered the eggs frequently. Wilmath went to Mary's to help with John as much as possible. While David agreed that she was a worker, he was continually complaining about the children.

One day in October, just after Ollie's first birthday, David confronted Wilmath about the little girl. "We really can't afford to feed all these kids," he told her. "Why don't you adopt Ollie out — she'd never know the difference! She's so small — surely someone would be wantin' a little girl and give her a good home."

At first, the idea seemed absurd — give up her baby! Why, the very idea! Wilmath dismissed the thought at once. But it wasn't long before David brought up the subject again.

"Surely you know someone who would take the baby and make a good home for her," he persisted.

Finally, Wilmath had thought of a plan. In November she boarded the train and traveled down to Love Lake. There she got off at the general store and, looking around, she saw old Mr. McCleary. He had come into the store for some goods, and Wilmath knew he lived out by the Cormans. She asked him to drop her by there on his way home.

Emma Corman was surprised to see Wilmath at the door. The two women hugged, and then Emma stepped back to survey her old friend. She saw that Wilmath had matured since she'd lived at Love Lake. She had filled out some, her waist was not as tiny, but the woman who stood tall and straight before her was still nice looking.

"Emma, I just have to talk to you — earnestly — it's very important!"

Emma sensed the urgency in Wilmath's voice and wondered what was on her friend's mind.

"You know that I wrote you about David — about his feelings towards the kids, especially Ollie." Emma knew that Wilmath had a spoiled, jealous husband and that she was trying to make this marriage work. So she merely nodded affirmatively and listened attentively to the rest of what was being said.

"Do you remember when I first met you, Em, and you told me then that you could never have children of your own — how much you'd like to have a girl? Well —"

"What are you getting at?" Emma interrupted.

"What if I let you and John adopt Ollie? You know you could afford another child. The boys are almost grown — your house will soon be empty."

"Are you sayin' you'd give Ollie up?" Emma asked incredulously.

"I have no choice! David may leave me, and I've already had a lot of problems with men. You know what I've been through!"

"I must say this all comes as a big surprise! John and the boys are out working in the fields, getting in the crops. We'd have to discuss this — you'll be stayin' the night. Maybe we can talk it over after supper — the boys will be tired and want to go on to bed."

John Corman and his two sons, Matthew and James B., came in at dark and ate an ample supper. Emma took her husband aside, speaking to him privately for several minutes. Soon the boys climbed the stairs and bid Wilmath a weary goodnight. John, Emma and Wilmath sat in the Corman parlor and discussed the adoption of Ollie. After learning that his wife still had a desire to have a daughter, John agreed to the adoption.

Wilmath wanted the conditions clearly understood before they proceeded. "I understand that Ollie will become a Corman, but I want the right to visit her from time to time. You will be 'mother' to her, Em, and I won't interfere with that. I will simply remain as your close friend, and I will visit here as such. She'll not know my true identity. I just have to know how she is getting along every so often."

The Cormans agreed to Wilmath's stipulations. Then John said, "I'll go down to Atlanta and see C. G. Buster, and he'll draw up the papers. He's our lawyer. We'll notify you when they are ready, and you can bring Ollie down here with you — sign the papers, and then she will be ours."

Wilmath slept fitfully that night, wondering if she was doing the right thing!

CHAPTER TWELVE

RIGHT AFTER CHRISTMAS, Wilmath received a letter from Emma Corman. The papers were ready, and she was to bring Ollie and come to Love Lake on December 29. From there, they would all go down to Atlanta the next day to Buster's office and sign the necessary documents.

The dreaded day came soon enough. She gathered up the few things the baby had and left Lottie and Jim with Paulina. David drove them by the Dennis' on the way to the depot. These two poor kids had no idea they'd never see their sister again for a long, long time, if ever!! Sadness enveloped Wilmath, but she knew she had to go through with this — she had to be brave!

The Cormans met Wilmath at the Love Lake general store and took her and Ollie to their house. John had already purchased tickets to Atlanta for the following day's journey. Wilmath ate little and had nothing much to contribute to the conversations the rest of the day. She only thought of what was ahead the next day!

They boarded the train bound for Atlanta. Wilmath held Ollie tightly the whole time, knowing she'd have little time with her from now on. C.G. Buster had the papers ready for both parties to sign, and the process went quickly. They were soon boarding the train back to Love Lake.

When they arrived there, Wilmath bought a ticket to La Plata. She hugged and kissed her little daughter, who was unaware of all that was going on, and then handed her, reluctantly, to her friend, Emma. Emma kissed Wilmath's cheek, and then the Cormans walked toward the livery, little Ollie now in the arms of her new mother.

Once on the train, Wilmath felt a heavy emptiness inside her very soul. She'd always keep in touch with Ollie and, after all, she was in the capable hands of her dear friend. Still, those thoughts did little to comfort her. When she reached La Plata, David was waiting for her near the depot to take her back home and, on the way, pick up Lottie and Jim.

When they got to Paulina's, Lottie asked her mother right away about her sister. "Where's Ollie, Mamma?" Wilmath made no reply and tried to divert the child's attention elsewhere.

Lottie asked again of her sister's whereabouts when they reached home. This time, Wilmath answered very softly, with tears in her eyes. "Ollie's not comin' back here to live with us any more!" Lottie started crying and was still doing so into the night when she went to bed.

I hope I've done the best thing, Wilmath thought, as she looked around the house, already missing her baby daughter.

If she thought Ollie's adoption would help her marriage to David, she was wrong! Things actually got worse. He'd started seeing another woman in the area named Melanie Palmer. Coming home late at night, he was moody and sulky — sometimes complaining about the remaining two children being in the way. Jim and Lottie spent more and more time at Paulina's. Finally, on March 1, Wilmath moved over to Paulina's and filed for a divorce from David in the court at La Plata.

April 26, 1901, the divorce was granted. Several months later, David married Melanie Palmer. Wilmath had done everything on God's green earth to try to make the marriage work — even to the point of giving up her little daughter! Now she faced another failure!

Every month, she tried faithfully to visit Ollie at Love Lake. The little girl was growing and was changing each time she'd visited. How she wished she could watch her grow up! Emma was foolish about the child, and she had everything she needed in the way of possessions and care.

In the early months of 1902, Seba Dennis was still living with the Thorns. He was also getting restless to get back to Oklahoma and settle. The territorial officials had, the past August, held a lottery for the land in the southwest part of the territory. There were 13,000 homesteads available, and 165,000 people had registered for them. The heat that day was so intense that tar oozed out from the pine boards on the platform that the lottery officials were standing on. However, the weather did not deter the crowd that was in attendance.

One day when Frank sent Seba to Leonard to buy some supplies, it was near noon, and he remembered the kind offer Cecilia Milford had extended to him at Nora's funeral. He believed he would stop and maybe take a meal with her and her daughters.

Cecilia was happy to see Seba and was already preparing lunch. "Seba, I'm glad that you saw fit to take me up on my offer!" The two girls appeared, and they all sat down to the noon meal. Cecilia asked Seba about the Thorns and Grandma Reid. Then Seba told them of his plans to return to Oklahoma.

"Is it safe to be down there — after all, that is where poor Nora was killed!" Cecilia asked.

"I have written the sheriff, and he says things have settled down a bit more there now. He said they still haven't had any luck findin' Nora's killers. We'll probably never know! I don't intend to settle in Woodward — I want to go southeast of there, maybe around Cedardale. There's a lot of land down there for raisin' crops and good timber to be cut."

As he was ready to leave, Seba decided that the oldest girl, Annette, stood out somehow from her other sister, Lila. He thought he could tell that she liked him a little, too.

Hesitating for a moment, before going out the door, he said, "Annette, if I was to ask you to come to Cherry Box for a visit with me and Rosie and Frank, would you come?"

Annette answered immediately. "I'd love to, Seba."

Seba Dennis found himself whistling a tune all the way back to Cherry Box — something he hadn't done in a long time!

The summer of 1902, Wilmath was making her regular visits to see Ollie. Lottie and Jim were still staying at the farm, knowing nothing about their mother's trips to see their sister. They had spent so much time at their grandma's by now that they almost felt like they were Paulina's children instead of Wilmath's.

When Lottie was six, she started to school at Blanket Grove School, northwest of the Dennis farm. She and Sylvia had been together so much that they were more like sisters than niece and aunt. Sylvia missed Lottie when she was at school — she and Jim didn't play together that much, as he was a boy and was outside with Earl a lot of the time.

On one of her visits to the Corman farm to see Ollie that fall, Wilmath met a rugged wood sawyer, who was cutting timber on some property of the Cormans'. He had come up to the house to eat lunch, and Wilmath learned that his name was Guy Deskin. He exuded an air of confidence, and she could see that he was "all man." The tall, slender man with dark brown hair and brown eyes was the "adventuresome" type — her type! They exchanged a few pleasantries at the table, and then he went back to his work.

Guy Deskin was still working at Cormans' the next month when she visited Ollie. This time he came in several hours after lunch and, seeing Wilmath there, he asked her if she would like to go down to the lake with him. She wasted little time saying yes to him. They went down and sat on a grassy bank to talk. She told him she'd lived at Love Lake when she was first married and knew quite a few people there. She hadn't remembered him living there then. He told her that he, his parents and siblings had come to Love Lake about a year ago from Brookfield in Linn County, and that they were renting a farm. Guy had rented a farm of his own that adjoined his father's, and the two men farmed together.

Wilmath never doubted for a minute that Guy Deskin couldn't take care of business. He had, she thought, the same type of spirit that Seba had always exhibited. Just thinking of Seba right then caused a deep stirring inside her!

One evening toward dark, in the chilly autumn air, Guy had taken Wilmath for a rowboat ride on the lake. As he was rowing, he had taken his coat off and draped it around Wilmath's shoulders to fend off the cool air.

"Wilmath, why don't we get married! I know we'd be good together — we've both got itchy feet — neither of us wants to stay in one place all our lives — we're rovers at heart!"

"Oh, Guy, I don't know — you know I've got children, and I've had two other marriages."

"Maybe I should go up to meet them and your mother. You say you've got a boy — I've always wanted a boy!"

"I have a daughter, too, and there is something else you should know — Ollie Corman is really my daughter! That's why I come here to visit John and Emma regularly."

"Well, then, if you moved down here, you'd be closer to Ollie, wouldn't you?" Wilmath agreed that living closer and being able to see Ollie more often would be an advantage of living back down there.

Guy came to La Plata one Sunday to visit. Lottie and Jim were dressed in their best clothes, and Paulina had prepared a hearty meal. After introducing Guy to Paulina, Lottie, Jim, Earl and her three sisters, they ate and visited. Guy tried to make friends with Lottie, but the little girl didn't feel very friendly toward the strange man. Jim and Guy, on the other hand, had become instant chums.

After Guy left, Paulina agreed that he was a man who knew what life was about and that he was also very attractive in a rugged sort of way.

On the next visit to Love Lake, Guy wanted to make plans regarding their marriage.

"Can't we just go somewhere by ourselves where we don't know people and get married?" Wilmath asked, thinking of all her failed marriages and that folks around there knew about all of them.

"Well, Willie, I imagine, since this is my first marriage, my folks might want to be there, but I'll explain the dilemma to them. I really don't care personally. I tell you what — I have a cousin, Howard, up in Des Moines. Now that's not too far away, but far enough for the privacy you're wantin'. How about makin' it the middle of this month?"

November 17, 1902, Wilmath and Guy boarded the Wabash to Des Moines. Howard Deskin and his wife, Marie, were waiting at the depot and drove the couple to their little house in a crowded neighborhood near downtown Des Moines. Howard had secured a minister, and Wilmath and Guy had only to get a license and be back at the house that evening to say the vows. In a matter of a few minutes, Wilmath became Mrs. Guy Deskin. She liked the sound of that name!

After getting settled in Guy's house at Love Lake, Wilmath went to La Plata to bring Lottie and Jim to their new home. It would soon be Christmas, and they would be starting their life here. Lottie was enrolled at Love Lake School. She still didn't have much to do with Guy. Obviously he, like John, preferred boys. Jim was the apple of his eye!

Wilmath went to the Cormans' to visit Ollie alone. There was no way she could take Lottie or Jim with her. Guy was a hard worker, helping other farmers as well as cutting wood. Lottie had made some new friends at school and was settled into her new routine. Even though the boy was still young, Guy took Jim with him whenever he possibly could.

Occasionally Wilmath visited with Martha Penrod, Mollie and Mira Dennis. She was careful to confine her visiting to the daytime, because Guy had made it quite clear that he didn't want to associate with her former in-laws, even though they were still somewhat related to his wife.

One day in April 1903, Wilmath had stopped by Martha's house and found her excitedly packing. "Willie, guess what! Seba has settled on some land in Woodward County near Cedardale! The land is free, but the territorial officials have ruled that he has to reside on the property for five years. If he leaves the land longer than six months, he has to give it back. If he decides to leave before the five years, then he can pay for it, as long as he's been there at least 14 months. I am going down and settle there close by him, and I think Mollie and Ren, Charley and Mira, and John and Fannie are going, too."

At the mention of John's name, Wilmath shivered! She'd avoided the man since she'd come back to Love Lake. He had moved over to Fannie's clear across the lake from where she now lived, and now that they'd be going to Oklahoma, it would be one less thing for Wilmath to think about. John hadn't provided a cent for Lottie's upkeep or Jim's, and she hadn't expected it. He'd made no attempt to see Lottie at all — Wilmath guessed he was engrossed in his life with Fannie and that suited her fine!

"Martha, that means that you all will have to stay down there at least five years. I'll be sorry to see you and Mira and Mollie leave this area."

"Yes, dear, but to get land that's absolutely free — that's quite a good deal! And most of the family will be down there. I will miss our visits, but you have a new husband and a new life." The two women hugged, and Wilmath knew it would be a long time before she saw the Dennis women again!

One thing soon became very clear to Wilmath — when things didn't go Guy's way, he exhibited a terrible temper. He also stopped occasionally at the tavern and had a few drinks, becoming intoxicated part of the time. But all in all, he and Wilmath seemed to get along well together.

The latter part of May 1905, Wilmath received a letter, along with a newspaper clipping, from Paulina. Her mother said that Seba had been courting Annette Milford when he left for Oklahoma, and they had corresponded ever since. Seba had promised to send for her as soon as he had his log house built on his farm in Cedardale. When the Dennis brothers had arrived two years earlier, they had helped Seba with the construction.

Wilmath picked up the clipping and read:

> *"Married at the Dunham Hotel, were Seba S. Dennis of Cedardale and Miss Annette Milford, of Leonard, MO. Rev. Long, officiating.*
>
> *The bride is one of Missouri's fairest daughters, and came to Cedardale only a few days ago to meet the man of her choice.*
>
> *Mr. Dennis has been here several years, and by his gentlemanly ways, he numbers his friends only by the persons he has met. He has made a home for his bride, promising to send for her as soon as that was accomplished.*
>
> *By his energy he has built a nice little home on his farm south from here, and after the ceremony, they left immediately for home."*

After reading the news, Wilmath sat down in the closest chair. What was it about these Milford women that Seba found so alluring! Well, if that was what he wanted, then so be it! She, after all, had a husband! Still, if she had been compelled to tell the truth that lurked deep within her, Seba's new marriage saddened her greatly.

In 1906 the Deskins' marriage was in its fourth year. Guy was having Jim, who was eight, help him saw wood whenever he wasn't in school. Lottie was still steering clear of her stepfather as much as possible. She knew Guy's temper got out of control, especially when he was drinking.

One evening after he'd been imbibing with some cronies at Love Lake, he came home to find Lottie sitting near a lamp, working on her studies.

"Well, missy," he sneered drunkenly at the ten-year-old girl, "isn't it a bit late for you bein' up?"

"No, sir, I'm workin' on some school studies," she said meekly, not looking up at him.

"We'll see just how late it is!" After saying that, he went to the barn and came back with a buggy whip in his hands. He lashed out at the child's back with the whip, making her yell with fear, tears flooding her face. Wilmath heard the commotion and hurried into the room.

"What's going on?" she demanded.

"Looks like your daughter here wants to sass me and tell me it's not too late to be up this time of night. So I gave her a little somethin' to think about!"

"Lottie, go get in bed," Wilmath commanded her daughter.

"You'd better go up to bed, too, Willie, or I'll be tempted to give you a few licks with this here weapon," he smirked. Wilmath said nothing. She knew there would be no reasoning with him tonight.

She went upstairs where the whimpering girl was lying on the bed, her back sporting two long streaks of red that were already beginning to swell. Wanting to comfort the child, she stretched her long arms around the little girl's waist and held her tightly, pulling her snug against her breasts. There was little she could say — whatever she said would make things worse. Hopefully, it would never happen again! She knew that Guy was restless — he'd been in one place for four years, and his drinking was getting out of hand!

She mentioned nothing about the incident the next morning, hoping the problem would go away.

Lottie went to school in the fall and noticed that a little girl had just started the first grade. Little Ollie Corman was chubby, with big brown eyes and an olive complexion.

"Hi, there," Lottie said to the little girl, "what's your name?"

"I'm Ollie Corman. I live south of the lake, and I have two big brothers," she announced proudly.

"I'm Lottie Dennis, and I live north of the lake, and I have a younger brother," Lottie said, pointing to Jim, who was sitting quietly at his desk near the middle of the schoolroom.

The teacher was ringing the bell just then, so the two girls had to sit in their seats, which were across the room from each other. Lottie sat with the fifth graders, while Ollie sat with the first graders.

At recess Lottie was outside the school playing with one of her friends, Beatrice Lale, when she noticed the little Corman girl playing with two other small girls.

"Beatrice, that little Corman girl seems kind of special to me — I don't know why!"

"Well, I really shouldn't say anything — in fact, my folks would skin me alive if they knew I'd told you about her!"

"What about her?"

"You really don't know, do you?"

"Know what?"

"That she is really your sister!"

"You can't mean that — my sister went away a long time ago. I never knew what happened to her. Mamma just said she went to live some place a long ways away and wasn't coming back!"

"Your ma adopted her out to the Cormans — that's all I know."

Lottie thought about what Beatrice had just said! No, it just couldn't be — still — the little girl would be about the right age — her sister was four years younger than she was. No, she just couldn't think that this was true!

When Lottie got home from school, Guy and Wilmath were sitting on the porch. She wanted to ask her mother about the little Corman girl and what Beatrice Lale had told her, but she knew she'd have to wait until Guy wasn't around. When Guy went out to milk, she decided to talk to her mother about the news she'd heard at school that day.

"Mamma, there's a little girl at school named Ollie Corman. She's in the first grade. Beatrice Lale told me today that she is my sister. Is that true? Is it?"

Wilmath had to hide the shock that was coming over her! She hadn't thought about Ollie going to the Love Lake School. She'd thought the Cormans lived far enough south that she would go to Atlanta to school. She wondered if Emma had thought about the fact that Lottie was attending the same school. Wilmath hadn't gone to Emma's in about a month, and the last time she was there they hadn't talked about Ollie's schooling.

I'll have to go see Emma right away, she thought. To quell Lottie's questions, Wilmath answered, "Lottie, you know that I told you Ollie went to live a good distance away. Now, please don't discuss this with the little girl — you might upset her!" Lottie assured her she wouldn't mention the matter to the little girl. Then, accepting her mother's answer, she went upstairs to play.

When Wilmath went into the kitchen, Guy was coming in with the milk. She told him about the incident at school that day. Guy's temper flared! He left the kitchen, went upstairs where Lottie was playing and grabbed her up in his arms, carrying her downstairs. When he reached the bottom of the stairs, she was crying and screaming loudly.

"I'll teach you to be such a nosy little thing," he threatened, as he headed for the barn. Once there, he reached for the buggy whip and, uncoiling it, he started lashing at the girl's back, causing more welts on her already scarred body. Wilmath followed him out to the barn where he was whipping Lottie. Jim had come out to the barn and was standing behind his mother, his eyes wide open!

"Stop that, Guy, you've done enough to her. Try to control yourself," she ordered. Guy stopped, and Lottie ran to the house and ran upstairs to her room. Jim followed.

"I think we better talk about your daughter, Willie. First of all, we can't have her here snoopin' around the Cormans and findin' out stuff she shouldn't know. And, I think you should send her away — find some family that would want a girl around. We don't need any girls — what're they good for any way — havin' babies is about all. Now, boys — they're different — they can work! Yessir, we're lucky we've got Jim. You better do somethin' before that girl causes any more trouble in this house!"

CHAPTER THIRTEEN

THE NEXT DAY Wilmath told Lottie to stay home from school. She put some poultices on the welts on her back. They looked red and very raw! They were an ugly sight!! Why, the child would carry these scars to her grave!

Wilmath went to visit Emma and told her about the incident at school and what had transpired between Guy and Lottie earlier in the week.

"Oh, Wilmath, I never thought to discuss the school with you when you were here last. We've been so busy here on the farm."

"Do you know anyone who would want a ten-year-old girl to live with them?"

"The only ones that come to mind right offhand are John's nephew, Bob Jansen, and his wife, Ethel, up in Gorin in Scotland County. They have no children, and she's always wanted a girl. I'd have to discuss it with them — it's quite a ways to go."

"I have to do somethin' quick, Em," Wilmath pleaded.

"I guess you could go up on the train and take Lottie. I could write a letter for you to take with you explaining things to them. If they don't like the idea, they could just tell you so after you get there. It's the only thing I can think of right off the top of my head!"

Emma sat down to write a note to her husband's nephew and his wife that would explain the sudden appearance of Wilmath and Lottie.

Wilmath went home and began packing all of Lottie's clothes and an overnight valise for herself. It would take a whole long day to reach Gorin from Love Lake.

Leaving early in the morning just before daylight, Wilmath

and Lottie walked to the general store and boarded the Wabash to La Plata. Once there, they transferred to the Santa Fe, which took them past Gibbs, Kenwood, Baring, Fabius, and finally Gorin. It was almost dark when they arrived. The Jansens lived several blocks west of the depot, and Wilmath was heading that direction, leading Lottie along the way.

Robert and Ethel Jansen lived in a neat little white house, surrounded by a white picket fence. Tall red hollyhocks grew on each side of the gate, which Wilmath and Lottie were now entering. They knocked on the door and were greeted by a man in his mid-40s. He seemed quite pleasant and friendly. Wilmath handed him the note from his Aunt Emma which explained the nature of their visit. After he had read it, Robert Jansen invited the mother and daughter into his home.

Ethel Jansen was a pretty lady of slight build. When she learned of Wilmath's plight, she was delighted! She had wanted a child so much, but nature hadn't seen the need to grant her that privilege.

After fixing the visitors something to eat, Ethel escorted the tired travelers to the guest bedroom. Ethel and Robert discussed the whole matter into the night.

"Maybe we shouldn't even think of adoption for quite some time — let's take things slow and see what happens first," Robert decided cautiously.

"Whatever you think best, dear," she agreed, "but you know, I've always hoped we'd have a daughter of our own."

"Yes, I know that, but we have to remember that Lottie's ten years old — she knows her real mother. We'll have to see how she reacts to all of this."

"I guess you're right — we don't know how the child will take to this change."

Lottie didn't know what to think — she didn't want to leave her mother and brother, but she hated Guy Deskin.

Wilmath tried to explain the situation to her on the long ride up to Gorin. "Remember, Lottie, you will soon be grown and have a home of your own. Guy has a temper, and he sees no need for a daughter. It wasn't right for him to use that buggy whip on you, but there's no stoppin' him when that temper of his flares up! I think these people here want a girl in the worst way — you'll feel wanted for sure. I just don't have the right home for you.

You can always write to me, and, Grandma Dennis will always be glad to get a letter from you. You and Jim have lived there the first years of your lives, and she misses you. Earl, Amy and Sylvia do, too."

Lottie decided she would give the Jansens a try — after all, it would unburden her mother!

The following day Wilmath boarded the train at Gorin early in the day and stopped at La Plata on her way to Love Lake. Frank Turner, who lived in the Dennis neighborhood, worked at the depot, and Wilmath knew he'd be getting off work about now, so she waited and rode out to the house with him.

Ma was glad to see her! However, when Wilmath told her mother about Lottie's new home and the episodes involving the buggy whip, Paulina bristled.

"Now, listen here, Wilmath — how in tarnation could you let this man abuse that child that way? She'll be as much scarred inside as she is on the outside from that kind of treatment!"

"I know it's bad, Ma, but what do you expect me to do — get another divorce? You know I'm considered the 'black sheep' of the family now. How would that look to folks? Besides, I think the Jansens will be good to Lottie and really grow fond of her. And, Ma, you know Guy thinks as much of Jim as he would a son of his own."

"Nonsense," scoffed Paulina, "Guy Deskin ain't fond of nobody but himself." Then she added, "Those people up there in Gorin better be good to my granddaughter or they'll have to answer to me!"

During the next six months, letters came to both Wilmath and Paulina from Lottie, stating that Robert Jansen was a kind, thoughtful man. He bought Lottie some material at the mercantile, and Ethel sewed up several dresses and undergarments for her. Later on, most of the letters centered around Robert, with little mention of Ethel.

Soon Lottie wrote Paulina that Ethel was extremely jealous of the attention Robert was showering on her, and it was causing conflict between the couple. Ethel was now feeling resentful toward Lottie!

"I'll not have my granddaughter living in another upheaval!" Paulina exclaimed as she read Lottie's latest letter. She decided not to discuss the matter with Wilmath. After all, she couldn't have Lottie back at Love Lake anyway.

The next morning Paulina awakened Earl, and they went to the La Plata depot where they boarded the train to Gorin. When they arrived there, they asked directions to the Robert Jansen home. They were soon standing at their door, which was opened by Ethel, who stared at the strangers.

"We've come to take my granddaughter home with us," Paulina's voice boomed out. Hearing her grandma's familiar voice, Lottie burst out the door and into Paulina's arms. Then she hugged Earl. Was she ever glad to see both of them! Robert soon appeared and asked about all the commotion. He shook his head sadly as Paulina explained the contents of Lottie's latest letter. Ethel remained silent and returned inside, where she hastily gathered up Lottie's clothing and possessions. Robert had asked the Dennis' to come inside while they waited for Lottie. Soon, taking Paulina by the hand, Lottie was ready to leave this house. She would really miss Robert, but she knew she had only been a "sore spot" between him and his wife.

They boarded the train, and Lottie slept peacefully all the way to La Plata. When the train stopped at La Plata, she woke up and, as they made their way out to the farm, she sang a rousing chorus of "Red Wing," with Earl and Paulina joining in at times.

When they entered the house, they were greeted by Amy and Sylvia. Paulina vowed that, from now on, she would provide a home for her granddaughter until Lottie was on her own!

Wilmath wasn't at all surprised to hear about Paulina's trip to Gorin to retrieve Lottie. She knew she was like Paulina's own. She felt relieved to know that Lottie would be with family from now on.

Life at Love Lake continued on an even keel, with Wilmath visiting Emma Corman and Ollie as much as possible and also going to La Plata to visit Lottie, Ma and her siblings. Guy wouldn't go along — Wilmath figured he didn't want to face Ma or Lottie, so she went alone!

In 1908 Wilmath's life was to take some unexpected twists and turns. On one of her visits to Emma's house, Wilmath learned that the Cormans had sold their farm and were moving to Kansas City to be near her brother, Edgar. Their son, James B., had already gone there to live with his uncle and had obtained a job as a bricklayer. Old John Corman was getting feeble, and Emma told Wilmath that they had decided it might be wise to move now, before she was forced to handle the farm work alone. The older Corman boy, Matthew, had gone to live with a cousin in Moberly. Wilmath was surprised, as well as shocked, because now she would have to go to Kansas City to visit Ollie. Her visits with the little girl would be less frequent due to the distance. She made Emma promise to write often and keep her informed about Ollie, who was now eight years old. Emma agreed to write to Wilmath as soon as they were settled, giving her their new address.

Wilmath received a newsy letter from Paulina in 1908. Vivian and her new husband, George Raines, were moving close to Love Lake. The sisters would be living fairly close to one another. She also reported that Victor, who had married a woman named Minnie, was getting a divorce and moving back home for a while. Wilmath thought that might be bad news because Victor had a drinking problem, and he seldom worked. However, Earl, Amy and Ma could use some help with Lottie and Sylvia still living there.

Wilmath saw more of Vivian after she moved to Love Lake. With Mira and Mollie Dennis and Martha Penrod in Oklahoma, and Emma Corman in Kansas City, she welcomed the company. In the latter part of the year, Vivian told Wilmath she'd received a letter from Earl, and things once again were changing at the farm near La Plata.

"Willie, Vic's movin' away from Ma's and getting married again. Earl wrote and said it was really a blessing! I guess Vic's been so liquored up most of the time that he'll do anything to get more. Why, Earl said that he was shootin' Ma's horses and sellin' the hides to get money to buy that rotten stuff he drinks. Vic'd tell Ma that the horses were just dyin' from some disease or another. Earl didn't have the courage to tell Ma the truth. He said he's just glad Vic's leavin' the farm. Said he wasn't worth a plug nickel for workin' around there anyway!"

Wilmath was sorry to hear that Vic was turning out like some of her other stepbrothers — they could never leave that liquor alone! Earl was different though. He, like Seba, was special!

In the spring of 1909, Warren and Mary Deskin and their children — Joe, James, Mabel and Jennie — decided to move to

Montana. Their relatives, the Harlans, had already gone ahead of them and wrote about this great parcel of land, whose eastern two-thirds was still unsettled. The Northern Pacific Railroad was the holder of millions of acres of its land grant. They were selling off acres at $8.56 per acre. Realty companies were also toting land for sale. Since Montana often experienced insignificant moisture to accommodate the vast area of land, the "Campbell Dry Farming Method" was being promoted as an answer to this problem, to lure farmers and ranchers to the area. Jim Hill, the great railroad promoter, had just held a Dry Farming Congress in Billings, which the Harlans had attended. The Milwaukee Road was also promoting land. The boom was on!

The Warren Deskins decided to purchase space in a freight car for $22.50. They would board the Northern Pacific at St. Paul and travel to Billings. They could take all their belongings, seed grains and some livestock. Guy wanted to go with his folks, at least for a while. Wilmath and James, he said, could stay with Paulina while he was gone.

"I can't be tied down with you and Jim right now," he told Wilmath. "I'll be back after I help the folks get settled. Fact is, I just need to get away and see some country right now."

Wilmath was hurt that he wanted to leave them behind, but she said nothing. She could be with Ma and Lottie that way. Jim wanted to go to Montana in the worst way. Guy told him he'd take him there after he'd seen the new land. That was a promise! Wilmath packed their things and headed back to the farm.

When they arrived at the farm, they were mystified by the appearance of a strange man who was tall, slender and had little to say. Wilmath soon heard Paulina's voice calling, "Come on in," and she and Jim went inside the house. The stranger followed, but still said nothing. When they were settled, Paulina introduced them to the unknown man.

"Wilmath, Jim, this is your uncle, Bill Moore. He's been livin' up at Ellen's at Wilmathsville, but Ellen's sickly, and she wrote and asked me if he could come down here and live."

Wilmath had heard of William Moore, but she'd never met him. She knew that he was 12 years younger than Paulina was, and that he was retarded. After their mother, Nancy, passed away, he had gone to live with Ellen. He was a good hand to have around the place, but was unable to function on his own. She guessed Ma could use the help, with Vic gone, and now she had Wilmath and Jim underfoot again, in addition to Lottie and Sylvia.

Bill Moore just nodded to them. He was a gentle man, harmless in every way. He shuffled slowly out, saying something about the chores that needed tending.

As he was opening the back door, Wilmath called, "Nice meeting you, Uncle Bill."

He turned slowly for a moment and said, "Folks call me 'Tump' — I don't know why. Just call me Tump!"

Paulina told them that Uncle Tump got his nickname because he walked and talked so slow. Soon James and Lottie, who were growing fond of their uncle, began calling him "Uncle Bump" when he wasn't around. Sometimes they played tricks on him, knowing full well he couldn't understand things as they did. Wilmath scolded them, as did Paulina, but it did little good. Tump seemed not to notice and would play with the children and have them laughing for hours!

Guy wrote Wilmath several weeks after he and the Deskins had gotten settled in Billings. He told her that there was a bustle of activity out there. Billings was deemed the "Gateway to the West," due to three railroads going in and out of there. Settlers from Scandinavia and other European countries were coming to Montana to homestead. New towns were springing up overnight. Most of the settlers were building houses of logs with tarpaper for outer covering. The Deskins were building a three-room log house just outside of Billings, close to the Harlans. Guy was helping with the log cutting. He described this new land as one of great beauty — the mountains, he said, loomed out majestically, encompassing the city and surrounding areas, and the clear streams were havens for trout fishing.

Wilmath read the words, wishing that she, too, could be a part of this exciting adventure.

She got an unexpected surprise a few months later. Seba had written Paulina, telling her that he was coming to La Plata for a visit. There was no mention of Annette — that made Wilmath wonder about her. Several weeks after the letter came, Seba arrived at the door alone. At first, Wilmath welcomed him with a handshake, but before she knew what was happening, he reached down and gently lifted her up in his arms, swirling her around and hugged her tightly. He let her down just in time to see Lottie, age 12, and Jim, age ten, coming toward the door.

"Lottie — Jim," he cried, as he grabbed each one and hugged them. "Remember me? I'm your Uncle Seba!"

Jim looked up at this tall, distinguished-looking man and questioned, "Uncle C.B.?"

Seba laughed heartily and said, "Well, call me whatever you wish — that's close enough."

Paulina appeared just then and hugged him and invited him into the house.

During lunch Seba started telling his relatives the news about life in Oklahoma. "Well," he cleared his throat, as if he was hesitant to begin, "I may as well tell you — Annette and I are divorced! She ran off with a fellow — a lawyer — that was handling a land deal for me. They are living in Arkansas now."

Wilmath could hardly believe what she was hearing! Why, with Guy away in Montana, she could easily divorce him, and she and Seba could be together like they should have been years ago.

She inquired about the other members of the family. He told her that Martha Penrod was living down there close to him and Ren. And Ren and Mollie had a little daughter, Ruby, and John and Fannie had two children, Roy and Flossie. Charley and Mira had gotten a divorce. Mira had tired of Charley's drinking and had left him. Good for her, thought Wilmath! Charley had moved back to Love Lake and was courting one of the Van Pelt girls.

Seba also told them he had acquired some land around Driscoll from a man who lived in Herd, Arkansas, and he was going to stop on the way back to Oklahoma to settle up with him.

When night fell and most of the Dennis family had fallen asleep, Wilmath crept downstairs and went outside. It was a warm summer night. She thought Seba might be out there, and she was right! He stood in the darkness, as if waiting for her to join him.

They walked, holding hands, down to their old spot near the crick. No words were spoken, as each knew what was in the other's heart and soul. They were soon touching each other familiarly, as if it had been only yesterday that the two people became lovers. They lay in the soft grass, savoring each other's body with an ecstasy and wild abandonment that had gone unattended too long. Soon after, they were gazing up at the stars, each contented after the fulfillment of their desires.

"Isn't it odd how things work out?" Wilmath asked.

"Hmmm — how do you mean?" he asked in return.

"You're free now — Guy's in Montana — I can get a divorce and we can be together."

"Oh, Willie — don't you ever give up on that? We've been through all that before. We can't do that!"

"But we love each other, Seba. We've never had a cross word between us. I can't get you out of my heart and mind. And we have our son!"

"Yes, my dear, I've thought of you so very often, and we do indeed have a most discerning attraction between us but, as I told you before, we must remain as we are."

Wilmath sighed, looking at this wonderful man, the moonlight reflecting on his handsome face, revealing a thick shock of dark brown hair and deep blue eyes.

"I think we better get back now. The others might wake up and miss us, and wouldn't that be quite the scandal?"

They walked back the same way they came — hands clasped tightly together, parting only when they reached the door.

The next morning Seba announced that he was going back to Oklahoma. He made Lottie and Jim promise to write to him, gave them all hugs, then departed. Wilmath spent several days trying to forget, and yet at the same time savor every memory of her nocturnal encounter with Seba.

Seba Dennis arrived in Benton County, Arkansas, and asked directions to the farm of Mr. H.O. Gann in Herd. Arriving at the farm, he was met at the door by one of the most ravishing females he'd ever seen! A blonde, blue-eyed woman, in her mid-30s, informed him that her parents were in town and would arrive home before long. Seba couldn't take his eyes off of this "princess." She was small and thin, and her hair was long — why, she almost looked like an angel!

"I'm Seba Dennis — I live in Cedardale, Oklahoma, and I came to see Mr. Gann about the farm I purchased from him recently in Driscoll."

The "princess" extended her hand. "I'm Laura Gann. My father has been expecting you, Mr. Dennis."

"Please call me Seba," he stammered, hardly knowing what he was saying at that point.

The Ganns came up the drive soon, and Seba tried to take care of the necessary business. When he got up to leave, he said, "Miss Gann, will you write to me?"

"Of course," she smiled, "but you must call me Laura." Seba hastily scribbled his address on a piece of paper and handed it to her. Then he bid them farewell.

On the way to the train depot, he never once stopped thinking about Laura. In fact, all the way to Oklahoma he couldn't get the woman out of his mind. He'd start writing to her right away as soon as he got home! Thus, a correspondence was started between the lady from Herd, Arkansas, and the gentleman from Cedardale.

CHAPTER FOURTEEN

JANUARY OF 1910, Guy Deskin appeared at the Dennis farm in La Plata. Wilmath was surprised to see him, as none of his letters had indicated that he had planned to return home any time soon. He seemed eager to leave the Dennis house, as he knew Paulina and Lottie weren't overly fond of him, to put it mildly.

"Willie, I came down here a few days ago, and I've found us a place to live in town in La Plata. It ain't much of a house, but knowin' you, you can soon have it lookin' great in short order. It's on Browne Street. I figured Jim would be startin' the seventh grade at the public school, and I can get a job outside of town at the saw mill."

Wilmath was astounded that the man had taken care of all the details of their moving.

Jim had come into the house, had seen Guy and ran excitedly over to him, shaking his stepfather's hand. He wanted to know all about Montana the very first thing!

"Hey, there, young fella," Guy laughed. "There's plenty of time for tellin' about that — we're going to live in a house that I've rented for us in La Plata."

Wilmath and Jim hurriedly packed their possessions, said good-bye to Lottie and Paulina, and were soon going down the lane in a horse and buggy that Guy had rented at the livery in La Plata.

Jim entered school at La Plata, and Wilmath busied herself cleaning and refurbishing the house in town. She was close enough that she was able to visit Ma and Lottie often. Now maybe they would be able to settle down once more. Guy seemed content, but at night he would often spin tales of Montana to Jim, drawing vivid pictures in the minds of both the boy and his mother.

Jim wrote often to his "Uncle C.B." in Cedardale. Seba always wrote back, telling the boy about the happenings there. One day a letter came from Oklahoma, and it was postmarked "Driscoll." Seba wrote that he had built a new log house on the land he purchased in Driscoll. He also wrote that he had married again! Her name was Laura Gann, and he had met her in Herd, Arkansas, when he'd gone there to iron out details of the purchase of the land from her father. They had corresponded since then and had been married in Cedardale on January 17 by the county judge. Then he had surprised his wife by completing the log structure, and they had moved to Driscoll a few weeks after their marriage. Laura, he wrote, was one of the most beautiful women he'd ever met, and she was soft-spoken and kind-hearted.

Jim sent a postcard to his uncle in reply to the letter announcing his marriage.

"Dear Uncle C. B.,

Was glad to hear that you are well and doing okay. We are all fine. Congratulations on your marriage. I wish you joy, and a big fat boy.

To Seba Dennis from Jimmie Deskin"

Emma Corman wrote to Wilmath, telling her that John had died and that she and Ollie would be moving in with her brother, Edgar. She would send their new address later. Wilmath wanted to go see Ollie, but the train fare to Kansas City was expensive.

April 5, 1911, a telegram arrived at the Guy Deskin residence in La Plata. Jennie Deskin, Guy's youngest sibling, had died in Billings from typhoid. The body was being brought to Atlanta for burial.

The Deskin family arrived in Atlanta on the train with the body of the young girl. Hershel Gooding, of the Gooding Funeral Parlor in Atlanta, went to the depot and transported the body to his establishment.

Water was a precious commodity outside of Billings where the Deskins lived. They had to haul it in tank wagons to their property, because well drilling in the rocky land was unpredictable and costly. The water problem caused many sicknesses and deaths of children there. Jennie Deskin was one of many of those that had succumbed to this malady.

The funeral was held at the Mt. Tabor Church east of Atlanta. Wilmath and Guy joined the rest of the family for the sad occasion. Mabel, the oldest Deskin sister, lived in Wardner, Idaho, where she and her husband, Otis Magruder, had gone to live following a rift with some of the family members. They had not come back for the service and burial. While reading the girl's obituary, the minister mentioned that an older brother, Harlan, had passed away in 1906. Jennie would be laid to rest beside him in the Mt. Tabor Cemetery after the service.

Wilmath learned that the Deskin family had become "divided" in Montana. Joe had decided to stay in Atlanta and never wanted to return to the state. Mabel had gone to Idaho, and James wanted to go back with his parents. She was even more surprised to learn that Guy had decided he was going back to Billings with his folks. He informed Wilmath and Jim that he would send for them after he had helped his parents, now that some of the family was drifting apart. It would be a while before they could get over the loss of their youngest daughter.

Guy packed and soon departed with his family to Billings. Wilmath and Jim once again went back to Paulina's.

There had been several family deaths during the year of 1911. Just two months earlier, Vivian had passed away at Love Lake. Paulina had lost another child! Early in February Paulina had gone to Love Lake to be near Vivian, as her first baby was due around then. It had started to snow, and by the time it had stopped there was nearly 12 inches on the ground. Vivian was 27, and Paulina had worried about her having her first baby at that age. On February 7, Vivian was in labor, but she couldn't seem to deliver the child. Charley Dennis' new wife, Armelda, was there assisting Paulina. George Raines, Vivian's husband, was doing what he could to help as well. When it became apparent that Vivian had lost consciousness and there was no way the doctor could get there through all the snow from Atlanta, they tried futilely to revive her. Finally they could see that the woman was no longer breathing.

It was the next day before Charley Dennis could get down to Atlanta to get Dr. Throckmorten, the coroner. Finally they had arrived at the Raines household and, after examining the dead woman, the doctor assured all of them that they had done everything possible under the circumstances. The baby had been dead for several days before Vivian had a sign of any pain, and she wasn't able to rid her body of the dead child. Charley helped the doctor load the body onto the wagon, transporting it to Atlanta to Gooding's Funeral Parlor. George wanted Vivian buried at Love Lake. It was almost a week later, after the snow had melted, that Paulina, Earl, Amy and Wilmath came to attend the burial of their daughter and sister.

In August 1912, Guy Deskin wrote Wilmath and Jim that he wanted them to join him in Montana. He had been working at a sawmill, cutting logs for houses, as people were still coming to the area to settle. Wilmath agreed to go to Montana, but she wanted to visit Ollie in Kansas City before leaving Missouri.

She boarded the Santa Fe at La Plata and rode to Kansas City, arriving at Union Station in the early part of August. Edgar Marsh lived at 410 N. Prospect. Wilmath had no idea where to go, so she asked one of the agents at the station there, and he told her there would be a streetcar that would take her to Prospect Street. She boarded the streetcar bound for North Prospect and got off near the 400 block. The area was industrial and near the Missouri River bottoms. She hadn't bothered to let Emma know that she was coming.

A short thin man greeted her at the door. Wilmath told Edgar Marsh that she was Mrs. Deskin, a friend of Emma's, and he immediately understood and invited her into the house. Emma gave her old friend a big hug, then ushered her into the sitting room where Ollie was playing with some dolls.

"Ollie, dear, you do remember my friend, Mrs. Deskin, don't you? She used to visit us on the farm at Love Lake." Ollie hopped up to give the pretty woman a hug. Of course, she remembered this lady who had always walked so straight, wore a big hat and smelled of lilacs. Pleasantries were exchanged, and after Ollie was sound asleep, Wilmath and Emma visited for what seemed like hours. Wilmath told her she'd write as soon as they found a place of their own in Montana. Presently Guy was staying with his cousin and wife, the El Roy Harlans.

On the second day of her visit, Wilmath was preparing to leave early in the morning. She gave Ollie a hug and kiss that had to last both of them a long time. Then she rode the streetcar back to Union Station, boarded the Santa Fe and went back to La Plata to prepare for the trip to Montana.

Ollie felt an odd loneliness after her mother's friend, Mrs. Deskin, had gone. Emma, sensing the girl's unhappiness, invited James B.'s stepdaughter, Mary, to come over and play with Ollie. Ollie came to the door, and the two girls made their way into the sitting room to play a game of marbles. Mary was two or three years older than Ollie, but the two girls played well together.

"Why are you so sad today, Ollie?" Mary asked.

"I really don't know, Mary. We just had a visit from one of my mother's dearest friends who lives in La Plata. For some strange reason, I hated to see her leave! She's so very nice to me! I seem to miss Mrs. Deskin!"

"Mrs. Deskin?"

"Yes, Wilmath Deskin."

"Well, no wonder, you silly goose," replied Mary knowingly. "It's natural to miss your own mother." Mary had no tact at all, and at times could be quite bold.

"What do you mean, Mary — you know she's not my mother!"

"Ha, I know nothing of the sort! I've heard my mom and stepfather discussing the fact that Grandma Emma and Grandpa John adopted you when you were barely over a year old. My stepfather remembers it well. It happened on the farm at Love Lake."

Ollie could hardly believe what she was hearing! Surely this girl was wrong! It was like Mary to be a troublemaker at times. Ollie decided not to pursue the matter further with the girl, but she intended to have a talk with her mother as soon as the girl left.

Late that evening, Ollie told Emma about Mary's revelation concerning the fact that she was adopted and that Wilmath Deskin was her real mother. Emma had decided that when the girl was old enough to understand, she would tell her the truth. Maybe now would be as good a time as any.

"Ollie, dear," she began, "what Mary told you is the truth. Wilmath was my friend when she was first married and had Lottie. Then she was married to another man who didn't want her to keep you. Knowing that I could never have children and that I wanted a little girl to call my own, she agreed to let me adopt you. She also insisted on visiting you from time to time, keeping up with you through the years. She has had more than her share of troubles. If she could have kept you, she would have."

After she managed to choke back the tears, Ollie said, "Now that I know, could I go see her — maybe spend some time with her?"

"Oh, I don't think so right now, Ollie. Wilmath still couldn't have you living with her. Her current husband, Guy Deskin, favors only her son, Jim. Her other daughter, Lottie, lives with her grandma on a farm in La Plata."

"You mean that I have a sister and a brother!" she exclaimed.

"Yes, they went to school a short time with you when you were in the first grade at Love Lake School. Lottie's four years older than you, and Jim is two years older than you."

"I can barely remember that girl — Lottie — she was nice to me, and Jim, he was rather quiet and shy."

All this news was a lot for Ollie to absorb at one time. She wanted to go to La Plata and renew her acquaintance with Lottie and Jim and visit her real mother — Wilmath. That sounded odd to Ollie — her mother was Wilmath Deskin!

CHAPTER FIFTEEN

THE FIRST OF SEPTEMBER, Wilmath and Jim boarded the Wabash at La Plata and rode to Kirksville, where they transferred to the Chicago, Burlington and Quincy Railroad. They traveled through Omaha, and on to Sheridan, Wyoming, and then on up to Billings. They had not seen much but farmland until they were close to the Wyoming-Montana border at Sheridan. Then mountains began to appear in the far distant horizon. When they got to Billings, they were surprised to see a city surrounded by the majestic peaks that dominated the Montana sky!

Guy Deskin and El Roy Harlan met them at the train station in Billings. The city seemed very crowded. She and Jim were whisked into the Harlans' buggy and were soon traveling on the eastern outskirts of Billings to an area where there were rows of log houses, all of which looked similar. When they reached the Harlan's house, they introduced Wilmath and Jim to Martha, El Roy's wife. After having supper with the family, Guy told Wilmath that he had been studying the country there in Montana, and he had heard that the area around Gallatin County was less crowded, and that there was a sawmill where he could work in Bozeman. He had, in fact, already secured housing for them there, and they would be boarding the train to go to their new home the very next day!

The house in Bozeman was on North Main Street. Wilmath decided when she saw the town that she was going to like living there. The Bridger Mountain range was just northeast of Bozeman, and one of its peaks was especially prominent, and the land was so natural and untamed.

Everything seemed to be falling into place again for Wilmath,

Guy and Jim. They had a new life in a new state — a fresh start. As she straightened her shoulders as usual, she exhibited a confidence she hadn't felt in a long time. She had left her other life behind in Missouri — she had a chance to be somebody out here!

After getting the house in order, Wilmath went shopping at the Bozeman stores. She found a milliner and bought a large hat adorned with plumes and jewels. Then she bought a fur piece to wear around her neck and a new dress and some gloves. In addition, she decided to go to one of the town's beauty parlors and get her hair cut and waved. She was Mrs. Wilmath Deskin, who made a striking appearance. Folks in Montana would perceive her in a different way than those in northern Missouri. She'd be a real lady out here, and she would be treated with the respect that a lady commanded!

Guy still possessed a controlling nature and a nasty temper, especially when he drank. Sometimes he even took Jim into the tavern with him — a mere boy of 15! Her Jim was growing tall and handsome — Wilmath found herself thinking of Seba again!

She received letters from Lottie and Paulina, and she learned from a letter she received from Emma Corman that Ollie knew of the adoption and the identity of her real mother.

After a while, Guy decided, upon receiving a letter from his sister, Mabel Magruder, that he wanted to move to Shoshone County, Idaho, to be near his sister and her husband, Otis. Wilmath wasn't impressed with her sister-in-law. The woman talked incessantly and said little of worth in the process. Wilmath felt she had nothing in common with Mabel.

Guy wanted to take Jim to Idaho with him, but Wilmath insisted that he stay there and attend school. He was in his freshman year. Guy packed and went to Idaho alone. Wilmath and Jim moved to a smaller house in Bozeman. At first, Guy sent money to them, then it came less frequently, and finally he sent none at all. Jim insisted that he quit school and get a job in a factory.

Seba still wrote to Jim. He also kept in touch with Lottie back in La Plata. Occasionally he wrote Wilmath a postcard with a few lines on it to let her know where he was and to keep in touch. Wilmath wondered what this new woman in Seba's life thought about their correspondence. She probably never thought much about it, since they were, after all, stepbrother and stepsister. Seba had written Jim recently that he was very happy with Laura, who was very elegant and stylish.

Wilmath felt angry — how dare he flaunt his marriage to this woman when he knew how much she loved him and cared for him! As she got ready for bed one evening, she reached far back in the drawer where she had tucked a picture of herself with Seba. She always looked at it before she fell asleep each night as she was getting ready for bed. Now, feeling more hurt than angry, she picked up the picture and ripped it in two — making two jagged separate pictures of each of them. She might have separated them on paper just then, but he had done worse than that — he had chosen to wed still another woman, but wouldn't consider marrying the woman who had faithfully loved him since their childhood days. Oh, Seba, she thought as she tried to sleep, why, oh why, couldn't it have been me?

Wilmath knew that Guy wasn't coming back to them very soon, if at all. All communication from him had stopped. Wilmath cleaned houses and did what she could to earn money. Jim was still working.

In the spring of 1914 she received a letter from an attorney in Wardner, Idaho, stating that Guy was divorcing her! Well, she'd not fight it! He wasn't supporting her and Jim and hadn't been around for some time. They'd manage! Evidently he planned to stay in Idaho with Mabel and Otis. She had a lawyer in Bozeman write to Guy's attorney, telling him that she would cooperate fully and wanted a divorce as well. The divorce went through quickly, and Wilmath found herself a free woman again.

Several months later, Emma Corman wrote her friend, saying that Ollie had insisted that Emma bring her to Montana to see her "real" mother. Wilmath thought this was a great idea. She would have a chance to see the girl, knowing that the circumstances would be different now, with Ollie's knowledge of the adoption.

Emma and Ollie arrived in Bozeman the first of October. Wilmath walked to the train station to meet them. After greetings were exchanged, they walked to Wilmath's small, but neat, house. Jim was at work, and that was probably best. That way, she and Emma could spend the time alone with Ollie.

Ollie had blossomed into a young lady. She would be 14 in a few days on the eighth. Wilmath thought a birthday celebration would be in order. The girl had grown taller and had filled out with a fairly full bust for a girl of her age. She looked so different from Lottie. Lottie was fair-skinned, round-faced, and had strawberry blonde hair. Wilmath could see that Ollie resembled Harley in some ways — mostly in her facial features.

She tried to explain to Ollie some of the circumstances surrounding her adoption — her inability to care for her baby financially, as well as a husband who was too jealous and immature to be able to tolerate his wife's attention being diverted from his needs to those of her child. She saw no need to tell her about her real father and why he didn't marry her. Instead, she told her that she, Lottie and Jim were all children from her marriage to John Dennis. She had then married a Mr. Reardon, who died shortly after the marriage. Ollie had taken the name of that stepfather, and when she had married David Blackburn, he hadn't wanted to change any of the children's last names to his. Why should she confuse her and make her more miserable by telling her the truth about Harley! Earl had written Wilmath a letter some months back, telling her that word had reached the La Plata and Gibbs area that Harley had married several years ago and lived in Arkansas with his wife and three children.

Ollie's 14th birthday arrived, and Jim and Wilmath decided that they would plan a special day for the girl since they had missed all her other birthdays. Early on the eighth, Wilmath, Jim, Ollie and Emma boarded the Northern Pacific. Only Jim and Wilmath knew their destination. They rode for several hours, heading west, then slightly north. Ollie and Emma noticed smoke emitting from the city of Butte. Wilmath explained that Butte was a great copper mining center, and the smoke was bellowing from the Anaconda Mining Company's smelting factories.

They disembarked from the train and got on a trolley which had "Columbia Gardens" written on its front. Shortly they came within view of the trolley turnaround. Jim remarked that they would be getting off soon at "the gardens."

In 1899, W.A. Clark, one of Montana's copper kings, had purchased 68 acres east of Butte and opened Columbia Gardens at his trolley car turnaround. It was one of the finest parks of its kind! It contained a scenic railway, a ferris wheel, a miniature locomotive and the famous "Carry Us All," which was a permanent merry-go-around. The gardens also contained a fish hatchery, an arboretum, aviary, roller coaster, canoe ponds, a zoo, arcade and biplane ride.

Ollie was excited and, upon entering the park, wanted to ride the carousel. The horses on the carousel were hand-carved, and there were 38 horses, four small ponies, and two benches. The carousel was 46 feet in diameter and had a Wurlitzer band organ playing melodious tunes. The children and adults who were riding the carousel were laughing and shrieking with delight. Ollie, Jim, Wilmath and Emma all rode the musical merry-go-round. Ollie and Jim rode several more times, in fact. Then the brother and sister rode the ferris wheel while Wilmath and Emma watched from the ground.

The place covered so many acres that they didn't have time to take in all of its sights. At the end of the day they got back on the trolley and rode to the train station — full of popcorn and cotton candy. Ollie talked about the day all the way home, telling Emma and Wilmath it was one of the best birthdays she'd ever had!

The second week of their visit, Emma was telling Wilmath that she was feeling some stiffness in her knees and joints, and Wilmath suggested that they take the train up to Boulder Hot Springs. Jim and Ollie decided to stay at home while the two women traveled north on the Elkhorn line of the Northern Pacific, arriving at their destination in a little over two hours.

In 1909, James Murray, a Butte millionaire, had become owner of the springs, and he had redecorated the hotel there with elaborate and ornate furnishings. The lobby of the Hotel May had a 12-foot ceiling with light globes of amber glass made by Tiffany's of New York. There were arches and fountains, resembling architecture of Spanish missions, and the outside of the hotel was stucco. The card room was decorated in a Chinese motif.

Wilmath and Emma were impressed with the resort, which reeked of elegance. They made their way past the huge enclosed indoor pool where people were sitting in corners relaxing and playing board games, to the women's bathhouse. They changed into the bathing attire they had brought, and soon both were soaking in the mineral-laden water.

"I hear these springs will cure just about anything that is wrong with a person," commented Emma.

“Yes, I was hoping it would help the headaches I often get and the varicose veins in my legs,” added Wilmath.

“How did you know about this place — have you ever been here before?” asked Emma.

“No, but I was told by several women in Bozeman that this is the place to come for ailments and to relax. It feels mighty fine in here!”

“This is a pretty lavish hotel — wealthy people must come here often.”

“Yes, I’ve been told that Teddy Roosevelt used to stay here when he was here in Montana huntin’,” Wilmath told her. “I think President Wilson has stopped here, too. It is a famous place.”

Reluctantly the women climbed out of the pool, went to change back into their clothes, and then went back into the hotel to eat a snack before boarding the train back to Bozeman.

The next day, Emma told Ollie that they needed to return to Kansas City. The disheartened girl didn’t want to go with her — she was enjoying the company of her new mother and brother.

“Oh, Mamma, can’t I stay out here with my real family for a while?” she begged. Emma wasn’t surprised that Ollie didn’t want to go home — she knew that a day like this might come. A deep sadness penetrated her heart, but she knew she must allow the girl to do the thing she was asking.

“Well, if it’s all right with Wilmath,” she said reluctantly.

“Yes, do let her stay, Emma. I imagine she will tire of us after a while and want to come back to Kansas City,” Wilmath answered, trying to make her disappointed friend feel better.

“I could go to work out here, too!” offered Ollie. Finally, it was settled — Ollie would stay in Montana. A tearful Emma got on the train and headed back to her home alone.

“I’ll write, Mamma, and I’ll be back home one of these days soon,” Ollie promised her adopted mother as she departed. Emma nodded and hugged her tightly. She hoped she’d see her again and soon!

CHAPTER SIXTEEN

WILMATH AND OLLIE spent the next few months getting to know one another. One day Wilmath asked Ollie, "What would you think about me writing to Lottie and asking her to come out here for a while and visit?"

"Oh, that would be great fun!" Ollie said, her eyes dancing with excitement. They would finally all be together!

Lottie was surprised to hear that her mother wanted her to come to Bozeman. She hated to leave Paulina. Her grandma could hardly do the work around the place now. Earl was still there helping, and Uncle Tump did what work he could do. Amy had gotten married to Herbert Crowe, and they were moving to Illinois to make their home. Sylvia was married and living near Sue City, Missouri.

Lottie was 18, and she was working for the neighbor lady just north of the Dennis', Mrs. Susan Dent. Mrs. Dent was confined to a wheelchair, and her grandson, Clyde, was living with her, doing the farming and the chores. Lottie cooked, cleaned and did the laundry for the old lady. She'd also taken an interest in her attractive grandson, who was several years older than Lottie.

It had been some time since she'd seen her mother; therefore, several days after receiving Wilmath's invitation, Lottie wrote to her mother, telling her she'd come to Montana for a visit.

Wilmath, Jim and Ollie prepared for Lottie's arrival with an air of enthusiasm, looking forward to the reunion. Ollie especially wanted to see her sister again. She had written to Lottie when she had found out about the adoption and that Lottie was her sister. She reminded her of the day they had talked at Love Lake School when she was in first grade. Lottie had written back with joy — grateful to hear from her little sister and to know what had become of her.

August 1, 1914, Lottie went to Bozeman to visit her family. They were waiting to welcome her, and she hugged her younger sister and kissed her, and then she hugged and kissed Jim. Wilmath vowed to herself that they'd never be separated like that again! Lottie stayed in Montana throughout the rest of the year — writing her grandma back in La Plata often and also writing to Clyde Dent, whom she was missing more than she ever thought she would!

Lottie had gotten a job at a department store in Bozeman — modeling and selling gloves. She had grown into a pretty young woman — her round face was quite attractive, and she had an almost perfect figure! Ollie obtained a job at the store tailoring garments for the store's customers.

In the summer of 1915, Ollie decided to return to Kansas City to stay with Emma again. Emma wrote the girl that she missed her terribly. Lottie decided to return to La Plata — Clyde Dent was missing her as well. He had written to Lottie, telling her that his grandmother was in very bad health. Both girls left together on the train, with Ollie disembarking at Kansas City and Lottie going on to La Plata. Wilmath was sorry to see her daughters leave Bozeman, but she felt they needed to do what they thought best. After all, Jim would still be with her.

February 1916, Lottie wrote Wilmath and told her that she was returning to Montana to live. Wilmath was pleasantly surprised and would be glad to have her daughter near her. When Lottie arrived, she told her mother that Clyde Dent's grandmother was very ill and wasn't expected to live long. She also had some other news for her mother — Wilmath was going to be a grandmother! Lottie explained that Clyde couldn't leave La Plata now, but when Susan Dent passed away, he planned to sell the property and put matters in order in Missouri; then he would come to Montana to marry her.

Two weeks later Clyde wrote Lottie and told her that his grandmother had died. He would be arriving in Bozeman as soon as he could get the business in order. March 1, Clyde arrived at Wilmath's home. Lottie hugged him and kissed him tenderly on the lips. They decided to get married ten days later. They rode down to Big Timber on the train and were married by the judge in the courthouse there.

The newly married couple lived with Wilmath and Jim until Clyde got a job working on a ranch just outside of Bozeman. He had received a small inheritance from his grandmother, and he had purchased a Maxwell touring car. He promised to teach Lottie, Jim and Wilmath how to drive. Soon he regretted the promise he made to the two women, as they had a difficult time handling the "new contraption" due to the operation of the clutch. Finally, because of their sheer determination, the ladies learned to drive an automobile.

In 1915 the United States was having a problem in Mexico. A civil war had broken out in the country between Carranza and Franciso (Pancho) Villa, the two rebel leaders. Trouble had been brewing between the U.S. and Mexico since a crisis in 1914. By October 1915, President Wilson had backed Carranza, and Villa retaliated by killing 16 American engineers at Santa Ysabel, Mexico, in January 1916. Three months later Villa had invaded New Mexico, killing 17 Americans. Wilson ordered General John J. Pershing to lead a cavalry force into Mexico to capture the elusive Villa.

July 1916, James Deskin enlisted in the army. He was sent to the 149th division, 41st division of field artillery. The war was still raging between the two countries. Jim remained on home soil, being sent to guard the U.S.-Mexican border.

Wilmath was so distraught at the thought of Jim being in danger that she took to her bed for several days. Lottie tried to talk to her mother, telling her that it would do little good for Jim if she stayed in bed. She needed to be strong for him! Wilmath rallied and wrote to Seba concerning her worry about Jim being in the war. Jim was all she had left of the beloved man.

Seba wrote to Jim, and he also wrote back to Wilmath, telling her not to worry — to be the brave woman he knew her to be. He also told her that his wife, Laura, was gravely ill and would probably pass on soon. Wilmath wrote Seba steadily after that. She was truly sorry to hear of this woman's bad misfortune, even though she'd never met her.

In the next month, Seba wrote Wilmath, asked about Jim, and informed her sadly that his wife, Laura, had died. He said that he planned to remain in Driscoll and was also managing his mother's place in Cedardale.

The last of September 1916, Lottie gave birth to Wilmath's first grandchild — a big robust boy! He was named Ernest Hubert. Then Wilmath received a letter from Ollie. She was dating a young man in Kansas City named Orville Curry. They planned to be married in December and were going to make their home in Independence, Missouri.

Earl Dennis wrote Wilmath and told her he was marrying a girl he had met on the train from Hoopston, Illinois. Her name was Laura Butler. This must be the year for marryin', Wilmath decided!

The year 1917 proved to be a year of change for the people of Montana. When the Enlarged Homestead Act passed allowing the settlers to develop 320 acres of free land in eastern Montana, the newcomers were not told that the Great Plains area had "wet" and "dry" periods. Every 20 years, the area produced enough moisture for dry land growing of wheat, alternating with periods of drought. The years between 1900-1917 were the "wet" years. By 1917, the dry years started setting in. There was intense cold in the winter — the temperature had been known to plummet to 25 degrees below zero! The log houses, covered with tarpaper and insulated with newspapers, were heated only with wood stoves. There was no indoor plumbing. Thus, Montana winters were bitterly cold and summers were plagued with severe heat.

In the spring of 1917 Wilmath received a letter from Earl. He told her that Paulina wasn't well and she was going to sell the farm and move into town. Earl was building his mother a house not far from his own in La Plata.

"Willie, I really think you should come home for a visit. Vic's livin' with Ma, but he's no help at all. He's out drinkin' most of the time, and his second wife divorced him," Earl wrote.

Wilmath left Bozeman and headed for La Plata. When she reached the farm, she was shocked to see how old and frail Paulina looked. She was even more amazed to hear that Seba was coming to La Plata in a few days. While she was sorry to see Ma in such a bad way, she was elated about seeing Seba again. She worked hard to get things in order in the house — baking and cooking the day before he was to arrive. She was humming a soft tune to herself when Paulina shuffled into the kitchen.

"Well, Wilmath, you're still carryin' a torch for Seba, aren't you?"

"What, Ma?"

"You know perfectly well what I'm getting at. You've been after that man for years. You might as well accept it — he's not gonna marry a woman who has been married to his brother. He's not gonna heap any more disgrace on this family. It's bad enough that you've been married three times already and were only married to one of your children's fathers!"

Wilmath wanted to lash out at Paulina and express her feelings, but she bit back her tongue. This would most likely be the last time she'd see her mother alive. Earl had written that Paulina's heart was bad. Now, Wilmath's heart felt not only bad, it was sad! She left the room and busied herself putting away some laundry.

That evening she sat down at the bedroom table, the old lamp burning brightly, and wrote a letter to Seba. She would hand it to him when he left the house after his visit — not letting Ma see her give it to him. She wrote:

"My dearest Seba,

I'm writing you to ask you to meet me at La Plata at the depot when I leave Saturday at noon. Don't mention this to anybody. I got a severe scolding from Ma today — she hurt my feelings mighty bad. She just the same as said that I am the black sheep of the family. But she has always expected me to do the hard heavy chores around here while those lazy boys just laid around doing nothing.

You and I can get married and go to Colorado and get clear away from all of our folks. We could always come back for a visit if we wanted to. Dear, Jim would have to live with us when he is discharged from the army. I worry about him so much — I pray he'll be returned safely to me.

Now, dear, you study all this over and be ready to leave La Plata at noon on Saturday and go to Colorado with me. If you and I love each other as we should, we won't stop for our folks or let anything else come between us.

So, dear, don't you disappoint me — please be there on Saturday.

With lots of love and kisses, sweetheart, as ever, your loving Wilmath"

She stuffed the letter into an envelope and wrote Seba's name on the outside.

She had almost given up on seeing Seba when he came to the farm Friday at noon. He looked haggard and thin, she thought. She understood he'd been through quite an ordeal — having a sick wife to care for. Paulina asked him all about the Dennis' who were still in Oklahoma. He told her that Martha Penrod was thinking of moving back to Macon County, and eventually he was going to move back to Atlanta. Ren and Mollie had a new baby boy named Raymond. However, the baby was nicknamed "Buck," as the midwife who had assisted Mollie was a Cherokee Indian woman, and when she saw the baby was a boy, she remarked, "You've got a fine little buck." Seba added that John and Fannie and children were returning to Macon County.

"I guess I'll be movin' into town before long — Earl's buildin' me a house close to his and Laura's in La Plata," Paulina informed him.

"I think that's a good idea, Paulina. Earl will be close enough to look in on you from time to time."

"Yes, and Vic will be livin' with me. You probably heard about his divorce. He has no place to stay now." Wilmath thought that if Victor wouldn't spend all of his money on liquor, he'd be able to afford a place of his own, but she mentioned nothing.

"Of course, Tump will have to live with me, too — you know, he'll have no place to go once the farm is sold, and he can't be on his own," Paulina added.

When evening came, Seba got ready to leave, and Wilmath walked him to the door, carefully placing the envelope in his hand and putting a finger to her lips, signaling him to remain silent. He kissed her lightly on the lips and was gone. I'll be with him tomorrow, Wilmath thought — I know he'll come — he just has to! Wilmath could hardly sleep that night, making plans that revolved around a life with Seba.

Saturday morning she donned a new dress, a big hat that she'd purchased at one of the better millinery stores in Bozeman and a pair of black suede boots. She had her bag all packed and bounded downstairs to eat breakfast and tell her mother goodbye. Paulina gave her a small stuffed bear to take back to Bozeman for Lottie's new baby boy. Wilmath hugged her mother longer than usual that day — she could feel the old woman's bones sticking out — she knew Ma was on her way downhill, for sure!

Wilmath coaxed Vic into giving her a ride to the depot. She knew he'd not tarry after he let her off, as he'd probably head directly to the tavern. It was 11:30 a.m., a lovely May spring day in Macon County. Wilmath looked around for a sign of Seba. As the minutes went by, Seba Dennis didn't appear. She began to worry. He'll be here — he's just running late! It was almost time for the train to arrive! At exactly noon the train came into view and stopped at the depot. Wilmath looked around frantically. Maybe he wasn't coming — she'd have to go ahead and board the train! He could still make it though!

She sat down in a seat next to a window. There was not a soul in sight at the depot. In a few minutes she heard the conductor say "all aboard," and the train started to move. Wilmath continued to look out the window as the train moved slowly away from La Plata, not seeing a thing — this time due to the myriad of tears that were falling from her sad eyes.

He's done it again, she thought — he's rejected me! Oh, Seba, how can you just toss our love away like this? Surely he knew they were getting older and time would be getting away from them. They were both single for the first time since their childhood — how could he miss this opportunity! Well, if he didn't care, then, she didn't either, she decided, as the train was making its way onward. But, of course, once again, deep inside, she knew she would always care as long as she lived!

After she was home for a week, a postcard came from Seba. It read:

"I'm so sorry, my darling. I just couldn't come with you. I'll always love you.

S.S.D."

CHAPTER SEVENTEEN

IN MAY AND JUNE when an ample amount of moisture usually came to Montana, there was only a small amount of precipitation in 1917. Hot, searing winds came with the dryness, and there was a great epidemic of grasshoppers. They came in blankets of dark clouds, consuming everything from crops to shingles.

Clyde and Lottie soon felt the effects of the horrible "hoppers" on the ranch. The area farmers held mixing bees for cutting and grinding lemons. They had been told that mixing lemon rinds with arsenic and mash and spreading that mixture on the fields would combat the grasshoppers, sometimes called mormon crickets. That procedure did little to deter the insects. Then the farmers built hopper fences; they used beaters; they piled the dead insects into piles and burned them. Roads were impassable because they were laden with several feet of the slippery dead hoppers. Train tracks were also covered with them, making it too treacherous to run the trains.

In the towns the dust and wind permeated every crack and cranny. By 1918, settlers were beginning to leave Montana in droves. Vacant houses had fallen in. The wheat turned brown, then black, and finally to dust. Banks went broke. The folks that remained were those that were hardy. They grew gardens and raised chickens and bone-lean pigs. They also kept a milk cow. Rattlesnakes and porcupines served as food, as well as boiled weed soup.

In 1918 Wilmath heard of a job as a cook at the Broadwater Hotel and Natatorium near Helena. Colonel Charles Broadwater had built the elaborate hotel and resort in 1889. Broadwater had originally thought the Northern Pacific Railroad would come through Helena. When this didn't happen, a line was built that went from Havre to Butte, called the Montana Central Railway. In 1905 the hotel was purchased by James Breen and Augustus Heinze. The two men made the hotel and spa a place of beauty and splendor.

The Broadwater contained an enclosed indoor pool and outdoor pools with bathhouses with hot water mineral springs. The hotel's windows were made of ornate stained glass.

Although most of the common people were feeling the effects of the depressed conditions in Montana, the wealthy were enjoying a life of luxury. Wilmath worked in the hotel's restaurant, which served some of the finest food in the area. She was also allowed the use of the mineral pools at the hotel.

In the spring Lottie had a baby girl. She and Clyde named her Juanita Gail. Ernest was two years old by now. Wilmath quit her job at the Broadwater and went to help Lottie with the infant.

Wilmath received a letter from Jim. He was in the army hospital with a damp lung and in the first stage of consumption. She wrote a letter to Seba, expressing her worry about Jim's health. Seba answered her letter, saying that Jim was a trooper like his mother, and he was sure that the boy would pull through.

December 1918, Jim was discharged from the army and was receiving disability due to his lung condition. Wilmath was eager to see her boy. When he got to Bozeman, she noticed that he had changed considerably since she'd last seen him. He had gotten more temperamental and seemed to be doing a lot of drinking. Wilmath didn't know whether to blame the Dennis' or Guy Deskin for this trait. He certainly didn't inherit it from Seba!

Jim moved in with his mother when he first arrived in Bozeman, but he soon got a room at the Bozeman Hotel. He had a disability check to spend now! He rented several rooms at times and had drinking parties, with wild women coming to the rooms at all hours of the night. Finally the government heard of his spending rampage and cut his disability payment in half. Then Jim moved to an apartment.

The Agricultural College at Bozeman was advertising for a cook, and Wilmath went there to work. She began spending much of her salary on clothes, shoes and hats. Dressing in style made her feel special and important. She read some books on charm and worked diligently on developing some social graces.

"Mrs. Deskin is quite a looker," one of the college professors said one day. And Mrs. Wilmath Deskin WAS a more suave and knowledgeable lady than the young Mrs. Dennis in the late 1800s and at the turn of the century!

April 1920, Wilmath received a telegram from Earl. She had a "feeling" like she always got when something was about to happen. When she read the message, her feeling proved to be right — Paulina Dennis had passed away at her home in La Plata. The burial would take place in the La Plata Cemetery on April 20.

She arrived at La Plata on the 19th. It was raining, and Earl, Laura and their little daughter, Regina, met Wilmath at the depot. Earl, who was driving a Model T, drove directly to Paulina's house. Victor would be there maybe, and old Tump. When they arrived, Victor was there but was passed out and snoring loudly. Tump nodded when he recognized Wilmath. She told him that she was tired from the long train ride and bid him good-night. They'd talk tomorrow when Vic was up and around and she'd had some rest.

Paulina's body, at Earl's request, had been taken to his house. One of the family members sat up with her body all night long, and they were all taking turns. Earl's in-laws, the Butlers, had come from Hoopston, and they took a turn as the night pressed into morning.

The morning of the burial, Wilmath was up and fixed breakfast and then went in to wake Vic. She had to try to get the man in decent shape for the service. When she'd finally succeeded in getting him up and dressed, he came in to have breakfast. She was going to talk to him about the arrangements, then she wanted to go over to Earl's and look at Ma before they took her to the cemetery. A graveside service would be held there. She fixed Tump something to eat, then he went outside while she and Vic talked.

"Vic, have you got any idea what will become of Uncle Tump now?" she asked.

"Naw, nobody's thought about that, I guess. I sure don't have any money to take him in," he replied. "Earl's gonna handle the sale of this house and Ma's estate, so maybe he has something in mind for him."

Wilmath made her way over to Earl's and looked at her

mother, who looked like she was sleeping peacefully. She took Earl aside to ask him about Tump.

"No, Wilmath, I really don't know what we're going to do with him. I am taking care of Ma's legal business, but there's really no one to care for him."

"Well, I suppose he could come to Montana with me — maybe there would be some kind of work for him out there." Wilmath had no idea what she would do with the uncle, but someone had to take charge of him.

She went back to Paulina's house and called Tump into the kitchen to talk with him. "Tump, do you have any idea what you're going to do now? Earl's going to sell this house."

"No, I sure don't — I have no idea 'bout that," he answered.

" How'd you like to go back to Montana on the train with me? We could try to find some work for you out there some place."

"That's mighty kind of you, Wilmath. I'd be much obliged."

"Then gather up all your things, and I'll go to the station and get you a ticket right away. When I leave tomorrow, you can come with me."

"Yes, that would be fine. Thank you."

Wilmath and Vic got in the car with Earl and Laura, and they headed toward La Plata Cemetery for Paulina's service and burial. She saw many of the old neighbors from Wilson Town, Gibbs and the area where she grew up. Charley and Armelda Dennis were there, as well as Martha Penrod, who was now living in Atlanta and not very well. John and Ren Dennis and their families had moved to Macon from Oklahoma. Seba, she learned, had sold his farm in Driscoll, as well as Martha Penrod's farm in Cedardale, and he was winding up the affairs of both places. Consequently, he wasn't at the services. Martha told Wilmath that Seba would be moving to Atlanta once he got things settled in Oklahoma. She also mentioned that Daniel Dennis had been transferred to the state asylum at Fulton.

Earl and Vic were standing close to Wilmath, and Amy came up to give her sister a hug. She was still living in Illinois and had come down for her mother's burial.

As the minister recited some scripture and had a final prayer, Wilmath thought of those who had gone before Paulina — little Orena, Pete, Rosie Thorn, Vivian and Sylvia, who had died in

1916 in Sue City. Ma would be buried beside Pete and Orena. The years had taken their toll on the Dennis families.

As Wilmath left the cemetery, she walked by Charley, Ren and John. All three men removed their hats, and she heard John say, "Howdy, Miz Wilmath," politely, as she passed by him. Her shoulders were straight, her head held high — she'd at least gained the respect of these brothers by now. Not that she considered that such a big victory! She'd probably see little of them after this, with Ma no longer there.

Just thinking about Ma being gone filled her with sadness, but at the same time she was glad that Paulina, who had been a workhorse all during her life, was finally at rest.

CHAPTER EIGHTEEN

WILMATH LEFT LA PLATA the next day after her mother's burial, accompanied by Tump. When they pulled into Bozeman a few days later, she went to her house, checked on Jim, and then went to see Lottie, Clyde and the two grandchildren, taking Tump along with her.

"Hello, there, Uncle Bump — I mean Tump," Lottie said laughingly, as she hugged the man. Tump merely mumbled some sort of greeting. Wilmath explained Tump's situation to them and asked Clyde if he knew where the old uncle might get some kind of work. Clyde said that Mr. Lawson, the farmer just west of where they lived, had been looking for someone to help him around his place.

While they were talking, Tump was off playing with little Ernest and Juanita.

"Ma, we're gonna leave Montana soon — with the war leavin' things so depressed and this drought and wind here, we've decided to go back to Missouri," Lottie informed her mother. They were going to Knox City, Missouri, to stay with Clyde's dad for a while until they could find a place of their own.

Thousands of other residents of Montana were still leaving the state. Wheat prices had been inflated due to wartime demands and federal price controls, but now in 1920 farm prices had fallen off sharply. There were shutdowns and unemployment in Montana's lumber and mining industries. Wagons and automobiles were rolling out of the area daily with all the family possessions tied to the car. The Red Cross and the state government could provide little in the way of help.

The first of June, Wilmath and Jim went to Lottie's to say good-bye to her and the rest of the family. Clyde had the old

Maxwell loaded down with their belongings, as well as their mattress which was tied to the side of the car. There was a water bag on one running board and a toolbox on the other. Wilmath and Jim hugged and kissed them all, making Lottie promise to write as soon as they reached Missouri. Tump was next door at the Lawson's, and Wilmath thought they'd better check on him and leave their address with the Lawsons, in case they needed to contact her for some reason.

Two weeks after Lottie's departure from Bozeman, Wilmath received a letter from her. She told her mother that they had returned to Missouri safely. But they had encountered their share of problems along the way. At Big Timber they had met up with a band of gypsies. They had run alongside the Dents' car, trying to steal the mattress tied on the side. The gypsies had a camp near the town where they had put on a show of sorts for the town's people. They had painted wagons with dancing bears chained to them, wore exotic costumes and told fortunes. Most people believed they were thieves, and some families warned their misbehaving children that "the gypsies would steal them if they were bad!"!

Lottie also wrote that they'd had several flat tires along the way, as well as a couple of narrow escapes on some steep grades where they'd had to pull off on the passing cuts to let other cars by.

In the late summer of 1920, Wilmath went back to her job at the Agricultural College in Bozeman. By fall, she had been given the job of supervising the kitchen in the college cafeteria. One day in early October she was summoned to the administration office of the college and asked if she would agree to go to the college in Missoula for several months to help straighten out some problems with the kitchen staff there.

Wilmath asked Jim if he wanted to go to Missoula with her, and he told his mother that he definitely did not! He was dating girls there in Bozeman, and that was where his friends were. Jim decided to move to another apartment shortly before his mother left to work at the college.

The college had provided an apartment for Wilmath close to the campus for the short while she would be working there. Missoula was about 200 miles from Bozeman — she had to ride the train a big part of the day to reach the city. She soon got settled in her little apartment and was again spending much of her paycheck on clothes and hats.

Due to the length of the trip from Missoula to Bozeman, Wilmath went to see Jim about once a month. On one of her visits during the long train ride on the Northern Pacific, she had boarded and was settled in her seat when she noticed the conductor staring intently at her. He wasn't too bad-looking either, being a six-footer with dark hair. After the train was moving, he came by and stopped at her seat. He stuck out his hand to shake hers.

"Hi, I'm Lonzo Garren, and who might you be?" he asked with a twinkle in his eye.

"I'm Wilmath Deskin," she answered. "Have I seen you on this train before?"

"No, Ma'am, I don't believe so. I'm doin' this job to help out a fellow who wanted to be off work this weekend," he explained. "I'm actually a brakeman." She noticed that he was probably ten or twelve years younger than she was.

"Where are you from?" she asked.

"I'm originally from Fletcher, North Carolina."

"My, that's a long ways away!"

"Yeah, I've got a big family back there. Well, Ma'am, it's been nice meetin' you. Do you live in Missoula?"

"No, I actually live in Bozeman — I'm just stayin' in Missoula until the first of the year, then I'm goin' back to the Agricultural College to work — I'm a kitchen supervisor in the cafeteria there."

"Oh, I see — well, maybe when you get back to Bozeman I could come to visit you and take you to dinner. I'm out on the train all week — I live over east of Billings in Hardin right now. I usually stay there on the weekends."

Wilmath could see that the man was polite — a gentleman through and through. He had treated her with respect and kindness — something some of the other men who were previously in her life wouldn't know about! Seba had always treated her right! This man's personality was probably much like Seba's! Thinking about him now filled her with sadness.

Her thoughts had trailed off considerably since Lonzo had asked to see her. Mistaking her hesitation for a negative response, the conductor had started inching his way up toward the front of the passenger car.

"Oh, Mr. Garren," she called loud enough for others on the train to take notice, "I'd like that!" He smiled back at her, tipped his uniform hat and made his way on through to the front.

When she got to Jim's apartment in Bozeman, he spent very little time visiting with her. He was hanging around at the hotel with some shady people, she learned, and drinking — staying out till the wee hours of the morning. Even though Prohibition laws were in force nationwide, there was still plenty of bootleg whiskey. During the day, Saturday, she had managed to talk to him and catch up on some of the happenings in Bozeman.

Apparently Guy Deskin had married a woman named Mae in Idaho and had come back to Bozeman to live. She had little interest in hearing about Guy, but Jim seemed to be excited about the news. He had always looked up to his stepfather. In fact, Guy had been the only father figure in Jim's life! Jim had gone by the name of Deskin, although his name was still officially Dennis. She guessed she couldn't blame him for wanting to have the same name as hers, as she'd been Wilmath Deskin for over 20 years now.

"Guy says he's plannin' to buy a ranch somewhere on the outskirts of Bozeman. Says I can come out and stay with them when he gets the deal through. He won't be after me all the time about my comins' and goins'."

"Most likely, he'll be needin' help on the place. That's probably what he's after," Wilmath warned him, knowing Guy Deskin the way she did!

"That's all you know, Mother. He thinks of me as his son, and I'm lucky that he does. My real father, old John Dennis, never came around or gave a damn about me!"

Wilmath said no more. Let the boy think what he wanted. He was the only link she'd ever have to Seba Dennis, but he'd never know that!

Not wanting to quarrel with her son, she changed the subject. "I see there's a couple of letters here — one from Lottie and one from Armelda Dennis — did you read them?"

"Yeah, Lottie mentioned they were gonna move to Hoopston, Illinois, to be near Earl and Laura. Earl told them there was work out there in a canning factory of some kind. And Lottie's gonna have another baby!"

That news didn't surprise Wilmath. Lottie seemed to be a

natural for havin' kids. They had gotten a letter from Ollie about a month ago, and she was having her second baby.

"Looks like my girls are havin' babies every year or so. I may have dozens of grandkids before long if those two keep on!"

"How do you know I won't get married and have some kids?" Jim asked.

"Well, don't have a whole house full. My ma was tied down with kids for years. That's all she did. There's more to life than just raisin' kids."

Wilmath looked at the letter from Armelda Dennis. She had written that Martha Penrod had passed away in Atlanta. They had buried her in the Novelty Cemetery in Shelby County next to her parents, John and Phoebe Reid. Wilmath had always thought a great deal of Martha and was sad to hear the news.

She traveled back to Missoula the next day, arriving there late in the evening. After she got to her apartment, she took off her hat and gloves and started thinking about getting a bite to eat. She was surprised when she heard a knock at the door, and even more surprised to see Lonzo Garren standing there, looking like a school boy.

"How in the world did you find me?" she asked.

"I looked at the tag on your bag — your address here was on it," he admitted shyly.

"I just got home this minute or I'd offer you something to eat. There's not much food here either, since I've been gone all weekend," she apologized.

"I saw a little restaurant just a couple of blocks away as I was coming up here. What about letting me take you to dinner?"

Wilmath was delighted — she'd welcome a chance to eat someone else's cooking other than her own.

It was the middle of December and the air was cold outside. She was glad she'd bought a new fur coat with her last paycheck. She knew how cold winters could get in this part of the country — it would turn even colder after Christmas! Lonzo held her coat for her as she slipped into it. Then they started down the street to have supper. This is really nice of him, she thought, and he's so considerate!

Lonzo told her he just couldn't wait until she got to Bozeman to see her again. She had "caught his eye," and he wanted to know more about her. Where was she from? Had she been married? Did she have children? How old was she? The questions were endless! She saw no need in letting him know the unpleasant past she'd left back in Missouri. So she volunteered answers to his questions that were half-truths.

Yes, she had been married once before, and she had a son, James, who lived in Bozeman. She also had two daughters living in Missouri and Illinois who were married and had children. She told him she'd originally been from a small Missouri town and that she was 31 years old. After all, he could see that he was younger than she. And anyway, a lady never told her real age — reading that charm book had taught her that!

"Now, how about you, Lonzo — I remember you told me on the train that you were from North Carolina."

"Yes, Fletcher."

"Well, tell me more!"

"There's not a lot more — my mother's a hard worker and a widow now. My father died several years ago. I've got three brothers and two sisters living close by our mother there in Fletcher. I'm 28, and I've never been married!"

"I'm a bit older than you," she mentioned.

"Not so much that it matters," the kind conductor told her, as he looked into her big blue eyes.

Lonzo told her that he was going back on the train the next day and would be back on his regular route from Bozeman to Billings. She told him she would be going to Bozeman for Christmas, and after that she would go back to the Agricultural College in Bozeman to work.

Lonzo came to Jim's apartment, where Wilmath went after she was through working at Missoula. It was a few days before Christmas, and she invited him to come for Christmas dinner. He was delighted she had asked!

Jim had told his mother upon her arrival in Bozeman that right after Christmas he was moving. Guy and Mae Deskin had indeed purchased a "ranch" about one and a half miles northeast of Bozeman, near the Bridger Mountains. Jim was going to bunk in one of the old sheds out back of the place. He told her that he was also thinking of changing his name legally to James Lee Deskin. Lee, he informed her, had been the name of Guy's grandfather Deskin, and Guy wanted the name carried on. Since he had no children of his own, he told Jim that if he decided to change his name, he should consider using Lee as a middle name.

Wilmath didn't really care. At least, now Jim might be part of a family and have a home there. Maybe that would bring some sort of stability to his life. She just wished the drinking would stop. She'd seen so many problems it had caused with the step-brothers, as well as her half-brother, Victor.

She resumed her job as kitchen supervisor at the college cafeteria at Bozeman, and Lonzo came every weekend to see her. Toward the last of May 1921, he asked Wilmath to marry him and move to the little house he rented in Hardin. Hardin was in Crow Indian Territory to the east of Billings. Although this would mean that Wilmath would have to give up her job at the college, she agreed to the proposal. She knew now that Seba would never marry her, so she would try to be as happy as possible. Lonzo would be congenial and have a steady job with the railroad.

June 1, 1921, Wilmath and Lonzo went to the courthouse at Billings to obtain a marriage license and were married there by a justice of the peace, H.W. Nelson.

Hardin, Montana, was a primitive place compared to the big cities of Montana, such as Bozeman, Butte and Billings. The Crow Indians were very civilized and had their own schools and actually had their own little settlement. Still, it was lonely for Wilmath. Lonzo, realizing this, arranged to move to Livingston, a hub for the Northern Pacific. He had requested a transfer.

In 1922, conditions economically in Montana became better. The rain cycle returned for a brief period, and demands had risen for metals, lumber and oil.

Wilmath had heard of a new Turkish-like spa and mineral springs located at Gregson Hot Springs. It was very elaborate, featuring floors covered with oriental rugs, parquet floors constructed of exotic woods, rooms paneled with mahogany and several indoor fountains. Most ordinary people couldn't afford to stay at the place, but Lonzo insisted that Wilmath ride up on the train and stay for several days, since he knew she was fond of the mineral baths.

In 1923 on a hot Fourth of July, Lonzo wanted to go north to Shelby, Montana, to see the boxing match between Jack Dempsey and Tommy Gibbons. Wilmath encouraged him to go — after all, Lonzo was a man with few desires, and she realized that boxing was the only recreation he enjoyed. Fights took place locally and were a popular sport in Montana. While Lonzo enjoyed these events, they were nothing in comparison to the fight in Shelby, where he had come home grinning ear to ear, telling his wife that he saw Jack Dempsey win the fight!

Wilmath had heard little from Seba. She knew that he had moved back to Atlanta to be close to his mother. Earl had written to Wilmath, and he had told her that Seba was married again! This time he had married a much younger Macon County woman, Dessie Blanche Sholl. Wilmath had no more hope of ever having a life with her beloved stepbrother, so the news had little effect on her.

Jim wrote a letter to his mother in Livingston, telling her that he was thinking of getting married. He had been dating a girl in Bozeman by the name of Grace Michaels. Guy and Mae Deskin had decided to move to Boise, Idaho, and Jim and Grace were going to move into the house on the ranch and live there. Guy had given Jim his old Overland car, which needed repair badly, and Jim, being mechanically minded, had fixed it. He now had transportation! He had also started working as a mechanic at one of the local garages in Bozeman.

Lonzo and Jim got along well. Of course, almost anyone could get along with Lonzo Garren! Jim had always come to Livingston to visit, since it would have been somewhat unpleasant visiting him at the ranch with Guy and Mae there. Now that they were no longer living there, Wilmath was anxious to see the place.

Jim and Grace were married at the ranch in 1925, with Wilmath and Lonzo attending. She surveyed the place after the ceremony. What they'd called a ranch was really no more than a few acres. The location had once been the site in years past of a slaughterhouse. Jim told his mother that the soil was very fertile due to that fact. The Bridger Mountains were very close, and "Old Baldy," as the people of the area had named the third peak of the range, was very dominant. It stood formidably above all the other peaks, able to support only little, if any, vegetation at its top, which was covered with snow most of the year.

"Mother, it's really wonderful here! The air's great, and we're far enough out of town to have a nice big garden and enjoy the peace and quiet. There are few people living out here yet. Guy Griffin's place adjoins this one and there's a couple of houses on farther up the road toward Bridger Canyon. There's the nicest little creek runnin' through the place — why, the water's crystal clear and you can even go trout fishin'."

Wilmath once again looked around the place. It didn't face the road, and there was a long row of hedge on one side and a fence on the other. The house had a porch and only two rooms. There was an outhouse close by, as well as a chicken house and two sheds. Across the creek was a barn. Guy Griffin's place adjoined the ranch on the other side.

The Garrens had to get back to Livingston, as Lonzo had to go to work early the next day. Wilmath gave her new daughter-in-law a hug. Grace was a tall, slender girl with light brown hair. She seemed like a pleasant young woman, and Wilmath thought she might be the one to get her son to settle down to a more calm lifestyle. As soon as he had a family and home to think about, maybe Jim's wild ways would be a thing of the past!

The next year Wilmath received a letter from Lottie, telling her they were moving from Hoopston back to Missouri to Knox City. She and Clyde had rented the Foster farm. She wanted Wilmath to come there for a visit. Because she was the wife of a railroad employee, Wilmath had a railroad pass which entitled her to travel free on the Northern Pacific or any other railroad that she might need to transfer to. Lonzo had to stay in Livingston to work, but he suggested that she go to Missouri and see Lottie, and while she was there, she might as well stop at Independence to see Ollie.

By now, Ollie and Orville Curry had four children — Mildred, Floyd, O. E. and Eva Mae. Wilmath arrived at Union Station in Kansas City, and the Currys picked her up and drove her to their home in Independence in their Chrysler. They pulled into the drive in front of a big two-story house, which was located near an industrial section close to the northeast limits of Kansas City. Orville had a job working there at an oil refinery. At least, he'd be able to take care of his growing family, Wilmath thought. This would be different from Ma's situation, but still, Ollie was tying herself down with kids already!

When she reached Knox City after transferring in Kirksville to the "Q" railroad, she got off the train and walked a block to the J.W. Dent Harness Shop. J.W., Clyde's father, had won a farm in a gambling wager. The farm was southwest of Knox City. He had decided to deed it to Lottie and Clyde. They would soon move from the Foster place to the new farm. Wilmath waited until J.W. closed his shop and hooked up his horse and buggy to drive her to Lottie's house.

Enroute, he drove by the farm he was giving his son's family. Wilmath was surprised to see how small the house was for such a big family! The two-room "salt box" house had several porches and a tiny winding stairway that led upstairs to one long slanted-ceilinged room. It was here that the Dent children would sleep. Noticing that darkness was creeping upon them, J.W. started up the buggy, and they drove to the Foster farm.

Lottie, Clyde and all four of the children — Ernest, Juanita, Eva and Mary, met them at the door. After being hugged tightly by their grandma, the children left the room. Once out of ear-shot of the adults, Ernest informed his two sisters, Juanita and Eva, that hugging Grandma Garren was like sticking your head between two big pillows. He was referring to Wilmath's more than ample bust!

Lottie's house was a fright! Little wonder! With the care of four children and the additional tasks of gardening and helping with the farm chores, all of Lottie's time was taken up! Wilmath went into the kitchen and helped her daughter fix supper.

Lottie turned and looked at her mother and said, "I don't know if I told you or not, Mamma, but I'm pregnant again!"

Wilmath, who had a nasty headache and stinging eyes, took off her hat, and in reaction to the news of a fifth mouth for the household to feed, gave her hat a twirl. It landed in the corner of the kitchen on top of a big crock of pickles that were soaking in a sticky brine.

"Damn," she said exasperatingly, "I never really liked that hat any way!" Lottie needed another baby like she needed a hole in the head!

After everyone was settled at the table and Lottie had served fried chicken, mashed potatoes, gravy and stewed apples, they discussed the new farm they would soon be moving to. Wilmath told them that J.W. had driven her by the place and, while it was small, at least they would have a place of their own.

J.W. had spent the night there, and early the next morning he drove into town to open the harness shop. Wilmath hadn't felt well on the train ride from Kansas City to Knox City. Her eyes were bothering her — maybe the coal and grit from the train was the problem. She should be used to it by now, as long as she'd been riding trains. Still, the trip had been tiring! She found herself suffering from quite a few health problems lately. Well, she guessed that was understandable for a 47-year-old woman!

Taking Ernest aside the next morning, she said, "Son, how about goin' out in the barn yard and collectin' me a little fresh cow manure?"

The boy looked oddly at his grandma. "Why, whatever for?"

"My eyes have been botherin' me ever since that train ride — I'm gonna make me some poultices to put on them — that'll fix me right up!"

"Well, okay, Grandma — whatever you say," the baffled boy replied.

He returned shortly with the fresh manure, which she dabbed on two three-inch by three-inch squares of cotton feed sack material. Then she placed one square over each eye and secured them with a long piece of material that she tied around her head. Two hours later she removed the poultices and rinsed her eyes in clean cold water. Why, she felt better already!

She played with the grandchildren and helped Lottie catch up on the laundry and tried to help straighten the house. Her visit had ended too soon!

Boarding the train at Knox City, her thoughts were still back on the farm family she'd just left behind. Poor Lottie! She was bogged down with kids, and she had little money!

CHAPTER NINETEEN

WILMATH WAS ABOARD the train which was just pulling into Des Moines when she saw the conductor talking anxiously to a man who had hurried up to the train as soon as they had reached the station. Soon, the conductor returned to the passenger car, telling all those aboard that there had been a huge train wreck just up the tracks and they could expect to spend the rest of the day, that night and part of the next day in Des Moines. It would take that long to clean up the wreckage, as well as to repair the damage done to the tracks.

Wilmath was disgusted! She didn't know what on earth she'd do in Des Moines all that time! The only people she knew here were Howard and Marie Deskin, where she and Guy Deskin had come in 1902 to be married. Why, they might not even live here any more. They'd be in their 60s by now! She remembered about where they had lived — it was near the downtown area. She got on a streetcar and headed down to that section of town. Although the city was much more crowded than when she was here before, she was pleasantly surprised to see that the Deskins' house was still standing.

Marie Deskin answered the door. Wilmath saw that she was much older looking — after all, it had been a long time since they'd seen one another! She and Guy had kept in touch with them until 1912 when they had gone to Montana. Then the communication had stopped.

"Marie, remember me — Wilmath Deskin — only I'm Wilmath Garren now?" she asked the woman. Marie, looking at the lady standing at her door, finally remembered who she was!

"Wilmath, dear, yes, do come in. It's been a long time." Wilmath was invited into the house — it looked decidedly different inside from the way she had remembered it. A feather bed occupied one corner of the sitting room, and an old man was lying in the bed, very still and quiet. He was looking up toward the ceiling.

Wilmath told Marie about the train wreckage and that she would be in town until the following day. The gracious lady told her that she was welcome to spend the time with them.

"Howard died two years ago," Marie explained. "Now my dad is very ill, and I am caring for him." She led Wilmath over to where the old man lay. He must have been 80 years old, and she noticed that he had been a big man once — his thin frame indicated that.

"Dad, this is an old relative and friend of ours. She and Howard's cousin, Guy, came here from Missouri to get married years ago. Wilmath, this is my dad, Seth Crawford."

Seth nodded and spoke almost in a faint whisper, "Did you say your name is Wilmath?" Wilmath nodded affirmatively. He asked her to sit beside him on the bed and reached out to hold Wilmath's hand with his old bony, gnarled one.

"Dad, you're not up to talking," cautioned Marie. "You know how it wears you out." The old man paid no attention to his daughter. Although he could barely see, he noticed that this woman named Wilmath was wearing a strand of pearls around her neck. They fascinated him! He started to talk — his eyes still affixed on the pearl necklace.

"Would you be from northeastern Missouri — Adair County?" he asked.

Wilmath nodded her head and said, "Yes, how did you know?"

The old man cleared his throat, trying his best to be heard. "Back in 1880 I was a drummer. My territory covered southern Iowa and northern Missouri. We lived in Centerville, Iowa, not far from the Iowa-Missouri border, and I peddled my wares to general stores in the area. One of my stops was at Mrs. McLean's store at Wilmathsville."

The old man was having trouble talking and breathing at the same time. His daughter was trying to silence him, but to no avail. He cleared his throat and continued, "I stayed at the boarding house in town which was run by Belle McLean. There was a woman I became involved with — I saw her whenever I was in town, and we were very much in love. One evening, I just left town — left her behind. I had Belle give her a strand of pearls, much like those there. He pointed to the strand adorning Wilmath's neck.

Wilmath was sitting on the edge of the bed, pieces of a long ago puzzle fitting together in her mind. This must be the man that fathered me, she surmised all at once!

He closed his eyes — his breathing became more labored. Wilmath was bent over the man now, almost hovering, her hand still clasped tightly in his. "If you can hear me," she said softly, "can you tell me why you left the woman you loved behind?"

The old man still had his eyes closed. She waited for his reply, and at first she thought he wasn't going to answer. Then, he said, "You see, I was married and I had a child — Marie here. My wife wasn't well — she'd had a disease when Marie was small — it damaged her brain. She hadn't recognized me or Marie for years. I knew I couldn't get a divorce with her in that condition, and I couldn't marry my sweetheart at Wilmathsville."

Seth was gasping harder and harder for breath. He laid back and once again closed his eyes. Wilmath thought he was gone. Then, after a moment of silence, his lips moved for one last time.

"I've never forgotten my Paulina!"

Wilmath was riveted to the bed — Marie was shocked at the news her dad had just divulged on his deathbed.

At first, neither of the two women could speak. Then Marie said, "I have to call the funeral parlor and make some arrangements. The undertaker arrived shortly, and the rest of the evening was spent making plans and notifying relatives.

Finally it was bedtime, and both ladies, weary from the day's events, went to bed, but slept little.

The next morning after having breakfast and helping Marie do the dishes, Wilmath thought she had better get to the train station. In a short while in this town she had known her biological father. Not wanting to miss the train, she asked Marie to fetch her coat. Still, both women were in awe of the news of the day before!

Then Wilmath said, "Marie, what we heard yesterday was a shock to both of us. I only planned to stop here and see some old friends. There must have been a higher power somewhere that destined me to be here, because I hadn't planned the visit!"

Marie, who had gathered her wits about her, said, "Wilmath,

you have a right to stay here and be at the funeral. You are certainly welcome to do that."

"No, Marie, I'll get on the train, and although we'll never forget what happened yesterday, try to think of him as being only your father. Because, outside of my birth, that's the only connection I had with him. You have been his only daughter all your life. You still are! You've been by his side till the end of his life. There's no need to do anything different now or mention this to another soul."

Marie, tears in her eyes, came forward and hugged Wilmath. As she went out the door, Marie said, "Wilmath, you are a wonderfully kind woman!"

Wilmath boarded the streetcar down the street at the stop and headed to the station where the train was ready to be boarded. The "wonderfully kind woman" cried all the way to Montana!

CHAPTER TWENTY

IN 1927 GRACE DESKIN gave birth to a daughter, Peggy. Wilmath went to help with the baby. The little girl had brown hair and blue eyes. Surely, now that Jim had a child, he would settle down. Wilmath knew that he was still drinking and hanging around with the "wrong crowd."

By 1929 the drought came upon the state again, along with the beginning of a nationwide depression. Problems intensified by 1930, and by 1931 at least 28 of Montana's 56 counties had filed for aid from the Red Cross. There was a steep drop in food prices, and wheat prices declined. Governor John Erickson had no solution to the problem. Mining companies in Montana shut down and the railroads, including the Northern Pacific, were in a slump. Lonzo Garren had no job!

Rex Garren, Lonzo's brother, owned a restaurant in St. Paul, Minnesota. He was in bad health and wanted to sell the establishment. Thinking that it would be a way to make a living, Lonzo broached the subject to Wilmath, or "the Mrs.," as he called her sometimes.

"Wilmath, would you consider moving to St. Paul — Rex's restaurant is for sale. You and I could buy it — we both know how to cook!"

Wilmath hated to leave Jim. Peggy was almost three, and Grace was going to have another baby. She was worried about Jim's behavior — some of the time, when he was drinking, he became abusive to Grace.

She voiced these worries to Lonzo.

"The boy's a grown man! There's not much you can do to control him now!" Lonzo said. She knew that he was right — still —

she had never lived that far away from Jim. But she had to think of the fact that Lonzo was out of work here in Montana, and they had to do something. Reluctantly, she agreed to move to St. Paul.

St. Paul proved to be quite a change for the Garrens. The restaurant, known as the Ninth Street Diner, was located in the downtown area at 229 East Ninth. The town was much more modern and advanced than the Montana towns they'd been residing in. Wilmath and Lonzo were going to live in an apartment located above the restaurant. It was the first time they would have a telephone. Although there had been telephones in Montana for some time, the Garrens had never bothered to have one installed.

Rex Garren lived in a residential area of the city and told the couple that they could stay with them until they got settled and got the apartment ready. Wilmath saw some needed changes to be made in the restaurant. She and Lonzo would work to get the place freshly painted and ready for business. As soon as the restaurant was renovated, they began working on the apartment upstairs.

In a couple of weeks they were in business. The diner stayed open every day from 6 a.m. until 9 p.m. each night. It closed at 6 p.m. on Sundays. Wilmath complained of her feet and legs bothering her, especially after a long day of work. They had retained some of Rex's former employees who knew the regular customers and how the place operated. It wasn't long before they were doing a thriving business.

Wilmath missed Jim and his family. She received a letter, close to Christmas 1930, saying that the Deskins had a baby boy, Lee Roy Deskin. Jim wasn't working much, things still being depressed in Montana. Wilmath wrote Grace that if they could leave the ranch, they could come to St. Paul and help in the restaurant.

In the next letter they received from Grace, she said that they had talked to Guy Deskin, and his sister and brother-in-law, Mabel and Otis, would move to the ranch if they wanted to leave and come to Minnesota.

In the early winter months of 1931, Jim, Grace, Peggy and Lee all moved to St. Paul. Jim drove to the city in a 1926 Model T Ford touring car. They had rented an older house not far from the downtown area where the restaurant was located. Wilmath was glad to see her new grandson, her granddaughter and, of course, Jim and Grace.

Lonzo and Wilmath worked the first shift of the day at the diner, while Grace and Jim worked the second. Wilmath watched the children while the Deskins worked their shift.

In the spring of 1933, Jim and his family decided to drive to Missouri to visit Lottie and Ollie. Wilmath and Lonzo hired Rex's daughter to help out at the restaurant for a few weeks while they were gone.

They stopped in Independence first to visit Ollie and family. The Currys had a new little girl, Delores, who was their fifth child.

Then they headed to northeastern Missouri to Knox City to visit Lottie and family. They had just crossed the old rumbling bridge over Troublesome Creek and headed into the Dents' driveway when a heavy downpour of rain began. Lottie and Clyde welcomed them, and once inside out of the wet weather, the Deskins greeted all of the Dent children.

Ernest was 17 now, and in his last year of high school. Juanita was 15, Eva was 12, Mary was eight, C.W. was four, Robert was two, and the baby, James, was one. Lottie had seven kids! Jim thought of what his mother had said about having a house full of kids. This small house was filled indeed!

Lottie prepared lunch for her brother and his family. Peggy was overwhelmed with all these new Missouri cousins. Her grandma had told her very little about her aunt's family.

It rained all night, and by the next day Jim told Ernest that he needed to go to town — he was out of cigarettes. Ernest told him that Troublesome Creek was out and there was no way they could drive the ten miles to town. Jim, undeterred by that fact, told Ernest that they would swim across the creek and walk to town. He and Ernest took off their clothing, swam across the swollen creek and put their clothes back on, going on in to town. When they came back, they went through the same procedure. Ernest told Jim that he must have wanted those cigarettes in the worst way!

The Jim Deskins headed back to St. Paul, knowing that the Garrens would be needing their help at the diner. When they returned, they were surprised to find a letter waiting for them.

Guy Deskin had written Jim, telling him that the Magruders were wanting to move back to Idaho. Guy offered to sell the ranch to Jim for $1,000. Jim was taken aback at the offer — he'd thought Guy would offer the land to him at the price he'd originally paid for it, which was $350! Jim decided that property might be worth more now, so he decided to sign a note for $1,000. He liked living in the area.

Jim and Grace departed for Montana, and the Garrens continued to work at the restaurant. Some people thought the couple made a strange pair — Lonzo was a man of few words. He and Wilmath worked quietly and separately, having few conversations. But that arrangement seemed to work for them.

Lottie wrote her mother a letter several weeks after Jim's visit. She told her that they were glad to see Jim and family, particularly since they had moved back to Montana and would be farther away now. Lottie was very busy with all the children and seldom mentioned anyone back in Missouri. This letter, however, was filled with several bits of information.

She told her mother she had heard that Victor had married again and was living in Macon. John Dennis' wife, Fannie, had passed away, and he was living close to Victor. Charley and Armelda were living in Arkansas. Lottie had only heard this news through the grapevine, as she never went about these Dennis relatives. Clyde didn't have much in common with some of the Dennis brothers, due to their drinking and lack of ambition. Lottie did keep in touch with Earl — he was the best of the bunch in her opinion. Earl and Laura had moved to South Bend, Indiana. There was plenty of work there, due to the fact the city was a major industrial and manufacturing area. Occasionally she heard from her aunt, Amy Crowe, in Illinois.

The last item in Lottie's letter concerned Seba. He and his wife, Dessie, were moving to Macon. They had two children — a girl, Lula May, and a boy, Olin. Seba had sent off for a watch repair course by mail. He had rented a house next to Victor and John, and was planning to operate a watch repair shop in a small shed in back of his house.

Sometimes Wilmath would receive a brief postcard from Seba, and he still wrote to Jim. She had thought that Dessie might not like the idea of her writing to Seba, so she tried to send a postcard to him at the repair shop once in a while. In the cards she only wrote a few lines — what was there to say — Seba now had a family!

The telephone in St. Paul rang in the wee hours of the morning on September 21, 1934. Wilmath had one of her "feelings" before she even picked up the phone, answering sleepily into its mouthpiece. It was Grace! She was sobbing hysterically!

"Oh, Wilmath!" she said, in between outbreaks of crying.

"Why, what's the matter, child — are you all okay out there?"

After some hesitation, Grace attempted to continue, "Jim's in jail — the sheriff came and got him about an hour ago. He's holdin' him in the county jail here — there was a murder yesterday, and they think he had somethin' to do with it!"

Wilmath was wide awake now! "Good God Almighty, girl — my Jimmy don't belong in there — he's not done anything!"

"I know, but they're holdin' him and four other guys."

"Surely they'll see they've made a mistake and release Jim, Grace. You call me and tell me what's going on there, or if I need to be comin' to help him or you or the kids!"

"Okay, Wilmath — it's just that I'm so upset — I don't know what to do!"

"Well, try to be calmer if possible, at least for Peggy and Lee's sake."

After hanging up the phone, Wilmath lay there, knowing she'd not be going back to sleep. She had no way of knowing exactly what was going on in Bozeman, and it was driving her mad! She wouldn't wake Lonzo — there was no point in doing that. She'd wait a couple of hours until it was time for him to get up and open the diner, then she'd talk to him about it.

Lonzo, who was easy-going and never seemed to get ruffled about much, told his wife that maybe she shouldn't make a mountain out of a molehill until she had gotten more information from Bozeman.

September 24, Jim himself called his mother. He was acting fairly calm, although Wilmath knew that he wasn't. "Mother," he began, "I haven't much time to talk, but I thought I better inform you of the situation here. They had an arraignment before the judge, and they are holding me here at the jail and charging me with murder! I'm in solitary confinement." Wilmath realized that her son was indeed in hot water!

"I think you'd better come out here as soon as possible!"

"All right, Jim, I'll have to arrange things here with Lonzo before I can leave him runnin' the restaurant by himself."

"I've got to hang up now," he said, as the phone clicked and the line went dead.

Lonzo assured Wilmath that he could manage at the diner. Rex's daughter would come down and help out. Wilmath had no idea how long she'd be gone, but she packed some clothes and boarded the first available Northern Pacific to Bozeman.

When she arrived at her destination, she walked several blocks to the jail. Even though her legs were hurting, she felt little of the pain. Her thoughts were centered on her boy's problems now.

Sheriff Lovitt I. Westlake was in charge of the Gallatin County Jail. He made an imposing appearance — he was tall with a thick neck and sturdily built — weighing about 225 pounds. He walked with an authoritative air, which was a necessary qualification for the duties he carried out as sheriff. He looked up from his desk, seeing an attractive, well-dressed lady coming toward his desk.

"Are you the sheriff?" the lady inquired, getting right to the point.

"Yes, Ma'am, I am — and you are—?"

"Wilmath Garren," she finished the sentence for him. "I have come to see about my son, Jim!"

"Jim?"

"Yes, Jim Deskin. I understand he's a prisoner here in your jail."

"Yes, he is."

Getting impatient, she replied, "I've come from St. Paul — I don't know what's going on here, but I'd like to see my son — so where is he?"

"If you will wait just a minute, we'll go through the necessary procedures, and then I'll take you to his cell!" Wilmath saw right away that the sheriff wasn't about to take any guff off of anyone!

After what seemed an eternity, she was led to the very rear of the jail, to the solitary confinement area where only the worst criminals were kept. The area was referred to as "Siberia." Jim was sitting on a cot inside the cell, and when he saw that his mother had arrived, he made his way up to the front of the cell.

Jim Deskin was five foot eleven inches tall, had sharp features, light brown hair and a long nose that turned up slightly at its end. He was extremely thin! While in the army, he'd had a tattoo of a girl's head engraved on the inside of his right arm.

"Hello, Mother," he said quietly.

"Oh, Jim, what have they done to my boy? Why, you've hardly got an ounce of meat on your bones — you look terrible!"

"Well, they weighed me in at 123 pounds — I have lost some weight!"

Jim walked back over to the cot, pulled a cigarette out of a pack that Grace had brought to the jail earlier, and asked a guard who was standing nearby for a match. When he'd inhaled a few times, he informed his mother of the happenings thus far.

"I don't know how things got the way they are," he began. "I just wish I hadn't ever gone to that drinkin' party over at Clarence Arnold's cabin. Four or five of us was drinkin' beer up there, and Clarence brought this new guy up to his place after we was there awhile. I didn't like the guy from the start. He was a war vet, just out of Fort Harrison — he and Clarence had been in the VA hospital there together once. This guy, Kelly, was a smart aleck and tried to make trouble for me. He was a union man, and he seemed to have it in for me because I'd worked as a guard during that strike at the mine in Butte a few months ago."

Wilmath could see the anger in her son's blue-green eyes as he talked.

He took a few more puffs and continued. "Grace wanted to go get some groceries, so I went home to get her. I took Clarence with me. Kelly stayed at the cabin. I had that shotgun that Lonzo had given me in St. Paul, because I was aimin' to hunt prairie chickens. On the way to pick up Grace, Clarence tried to get me to 'soak' the gun so that we could buy a gallon of whiskey. When I got to the house, Grace saw that I'd been drinkin' a lot and asked me to take the gun to Guy Griffin's and let him keep it for me until I sobered up. I went over to Guy's, left the gun, and took Grace to get groceries. Clarence went along and when we got back to the house with the groceries, me and Grace had a little tiff, and I told Clarence to take the car and drive on home. I stayed home the rest of the time, went to bed, and the next thing I knew, the police were at the door and hauled me here to the jail. I know I was pretty drunk that day, but I know I didn't kill anybody. I'm not sure what happened, but I think Clarence will try to set me up to take the rap for this thing!"

Jim was wiping sweat off his brow, as he stubbed the cigarette out.

"I know you couldn't have killed anyone, son — I know you are innocent. How about a lawyer — do you have one working for you yet?"

"I've got two lawyers — H.B. Landoe and James H. Morrow, Jr. They're supposed to be good defense attorneys. Old Fred Lay, the county attorney, is gonna go after me — he's gonna hang me if he has his way! Or at least put me in prison for the rest of my life! He's hot on my trail all right!"

"Now, son, let's don't think that way — nobody's gonna hang my boy or put him away! I'm sure when it comes to it, the jury will see that you get a fair trial — they'll see that you are innocent — I just know they will!"

Their conversation was halted by Sheriff Westlake as he came into the area and told Wilmath that she'd have to leave now. "Your time with the prisoner is up, Ma'am," he informed her. He had escorted Wilmath down the hall, past a row of cells, and soon she was standing before an outside door. He opened it for her, and she stood out in the crisp fall air, wondering how she'd get up to the ranch. Jim and Grace had no phone up there — Grace had called her the day of Jim's arrest from town.

CHAPTER TWENTY-ONE

WILMATH DECIDED to start walking north toward the edge of town. Her legs were hurting profusely now as she trudged along the street, making her way up north on Rouse toward the direction of the ranch. She'd walked about a quarter of a mile when a car stopped beside her. Wilmath didn't recognize the driver at first. When he rolled down the window and leaned his head out, she saw that it was Jim's neighbor, Guy Griffin.

"Hello," he called, "I'm Jim's neighbor, Guy Griffin. Do you remember meeting me, Mrs. Garren?"

"Yes, I certainly do, Mr. Griffin — how are you?"

"You're headin' up to Jim's now, aren't you?"

"Yes — could you take me on up there?"

"I was just going to ask you to hop into the car — that's where I'm headed!" Guy Griffin wanted to talk to Jim's mother, and this would give him the opportunity!

They were almost to Jim's house, when Guy initiated the conversation. "Mrs. Garren, are you aware of how much trouble your son is in?"

"I've just come from St. Paul, and I stopped at the jail and visited with him. I'm going to talk with Grace as soon as I get up to the house."

"Well, I tell you — they've really put me through the wringer here — them law men have badgered me and questioned me ever since the evening of the murder. They wouldn't release me until they were convinced I had nothin' to do with it. Did you know that I had Jim's shotgun in my possession?"

"Yes, Jim just told me there at the jail that he had brought the gun for you to keep for him because Grace had thought he had no business with it since he'd been drinkin'."

Guy had pulled into the Deskin drive by now and stopped the car. He shut the motor off to continue his conversation with her. "Jim came over last Thursday afternoon with the gun. He'd been drinkin' a lot — he asked me to keep it for him. I was out at the hog pen with George Hoell and his wife when Jim came staggerin' across the potato patch with the gun. I really didn't want to keep it, but I didn't want anyone getting hurt, so I did. Then I saw him drivin' up toward town with Grace and another fellow in the car. He said he had to take her to get groceries. Peggy and Lee had been over here all afternoon playin' with my boy, Ted. It got to be suppertime, and Eula, my wife, had food on the table, so we invited the kids to eat with us. Jim came over about nine o'clock and took them home.

"It appeared that everyone was sleepin' sound, until all the racket started over there about four in the mornin'. The police were bangin' on Jim's door, yellin' his name, loud enough for the whole neighborhood to hear. Then, I saw the sheriff handcuff him and put him in the car and drive off with him in the back seat.

"Later that day, some deputies came knockin' at my door, askin' me if I knew anything about the gun. They'd searched Jim's house tryin' to find it, and somehow George Hoell told them about Jim comin' over here that evening and askin' me to keep the gun for him. I went and got Jim's gun and gave it to them, and they took me down to the jail and have been after me ever since! I told them I didn't know nothin' about it bein' involved in a murder — I was just keepin' the gun like Jim asked me to!"

Wilmath listened as the man related the happenings that had occurred after the incident. Added to what Jim had told her, it made a sordid story!

Grace, Peggy and Lee were all standing at the door while she and Guy were talking in the car. "Thanks for the ride, Mr. Griffin — I'm so very sorry about all of this. I must go talk with Grace and the children now though." She opened the car door and headed for the house. Guy Griffin drove back toward his place.

Grace embraced her mother-in-law, and Peggy and Lee each received a hug and kiss from their grandmother. Grace and Wilmath had tears in their eyes. They said nothing about the problem just then, not wanting to discuss a thing of this nature in front of the children. Finally Grace talked them into going into the other room to play so the two adults could talk.

"It looks like Jim's got a pretty tough problem, here, Grace," she began.

Grace was upset and had trouble controlling her quavering voice. "It's bad, Wilmath — really awful! They let all the guys out on $500 bonds, and that Clarence Arnold is going to do him in, I'm afraid. You can't imagine all the things those police have been lookin' into since Thursday. They came and got Jim's clothes and shoes and even impounded our car! And they're sayin' that the gun Jim took to Griffins' that evening is the murder weapon!"

"Yes, Mr. Griffin was just tellin' me all about it. I was walkin' up here, and he picked me up and drove me the rest of the way. They've really put him through the mill. What do you think, Grace — do you think Jim could have killed a man — I know he had been drinkin' quite a bit that day, but I can't believe he could have done that!"

"Well, he says he didn't! He'd had a lot to drink when he showed up here, because I asked him to take that gun to Guy till he sobered up. I didn't want him to get into any trouble with it. He took me to get groceries, and when we got home, we had a little fuss. We made up, then we had some soup, he went to Guy's to get the kids, and we went to bed. Next thing I knew, the sheriff was beatin' on our door and callin' Jim's name. They said they were gonna question him in connection with a shootin' that had happened that evening, and then, they took him away to the jail."

She put her arm around Grace and tried to comfort the young woman. "Honey, don't you worry — we're gonna get through this thing. Nobody's gonna pin a murder wrap on our Jim!"

Grace's sister came to stay with the children the next day, and Grace and Wilmath drove to the jail to see Jim. When they got there, he appeared to be unruffled, had shaved and was reading a magazine.

"They say the trial by jury will begin about November 21," he told his wife and mother.

"I hope those lawyers of yours know what they're doin', son," Wilmath said. "I'll need to go back to St. Paul right away and talk with Lonzo and get some more of my things, because I intend to be here for that trial! You'll need me, and Grace and the kids will, too!"

Jim and Grace had a feeling that she was right!

Wilmath came to Bozeman several days before Jim's trial. She wanted to visit him, and she wanted to spend some time with her grandchildren. The November weather in Bozeman could act up this time of year. Tuesday, November 20, the day before the trial, the town was hit by a snowstorm. It was almost a blizzard! Wilmath went to the jail that day and wondered if she'd be able to get back up to the ranch!

Jim appeared to be weathering the anticipation of the first day of trial well. He smiled as he saw his mother being led by Sheriff Westlake to his cell in Siberia. "I'm glad you're here, Mother!"

"I wouldn't be anywhere else, with all that's goin' on here with you! Lonzo said to tell you that he'll be thinkin' of you and that he knows that you are innocent!"

"The snow's sure comin' down out there, isn't it? I heard somethin' about a big storm."

"Yes, it's a bad day out — it's lucky I came a little ahead of time, and it's still luckier that Grace's sister got up here before this weather kicked up." The sister was staying with Lee and Peggy while the trial was going on.

"Have your lawyers given you their opinion about the outcome of this case?"

"Not really — they just said they think the jury'll give me the benefit of the doubt — at least that's what they're hopin'."

"Well, I'm sure you'll come out of this mess okay. I'm just so sorry you have to be put through it all!"

It was soon time for Wilmath to leave. She tried to kiss her son through the bars of the cell. "Remember, I love you, son — no matter what happens, I'll stick by you!"

"I know that, Mother, and I'll get through this thing easier with you here." They said their good-byes, and Wilmath made her way out of the jail and out to the street. Grace's sister was waiting in the car to take her back to the ranch.

By the time the trial preliminaries began the next day, ironically the snow had mostly melted. The temperature was 39 degrees when Wilmath and Grace entered the courthouse at 9:30 a.m. A crowd had already filled the courtroom, and standing room was at a premium. There were two rows of chairs placed around the inside railing. Grace and Wilmath were seated in the first row. Finally a second row of chairs was placed along the wall opposite where the jury would sit, to accommodate all the spectators.

Grace would be allowed to stay in the room during the preliminaries, but once evidence was introduced she would be barred from the courtroom. She had been sworn in as a witness for the defense. Wilmath could remain in the room, as she wasn't going to testify.

The process of selecting 12 men to comprise the jury took most of the morning and part of the afternoon. In fact, it was 3 p.m. before the jury was sworn in and the trial started. Judge Benjamin E. Berg of the Sixth District Court was presiding.

County attorney, Fred Lay, made the opening statement, assisted by Walter Aiken, city attorney. They presented the state's version of the case and ended up asking the jury to convict James Deskin of murder in the first degree and send him to the gallows for killing William Kelly on September 20, 1934.

The defense attorneys, H.B. Landoe and James H. Morrow, Jr., asked the jury to be free from prejudice and be willing to give the defendant the benefit of any reasonable doubt.

The first witness to testify for the state was Robert Phillips. He had found William Kelly's dead body lying in Keggie Lane while he and another youth and two girls were riding around out by the "lovers' lane" near the golf course on Sour Dough Road on the night of September 20. The discovery was made at 9:30 p.m., and the youths went directly to the police station to report the incident.

Police officer Alfred Anderson then testified that he and undersheriff, C.H. Isbell, had arrived at the scene at 10 p.m. Isbell returned to town for other officers and the coroner. Anderson stayed at the site so that nothing would be disturbed. Anderson said that the body was lying on its back with arms spread, and the face was dirty, as though the victim had fallen on his face and was then turned over. There was a puddle of blood under the head and shoulders of the dead man.

A shotgun shell found near the scene and two pencils picked up near the dead body were admitted as evidence. Photos of Kelly's body were mentioned, but were not entered as evidence at that time.

The trial that day was finished by 5 p.m. Throughout the day Jim had shown little emotion — just merely a passing interest in the day's proceedings.

Spectators and attorneys agreed that the real excitement would take place when the state decided to put Clarence Arnold on the stand, as he was their only witness to the crime.

November 22, the second day of the trial, 11 witnesses took the stand, one of them twice. Clarence Arnold's whereabouts was not divulged, but the county attorney assured the court he'd appear when the time came for him to testify. Twenty-nine exhibits were issued by the state, but only two dozen were admitted as exhibits. These included: 13 photographs, the shotgun, the 39 pellets extracted from Kelly's head, Kelly's shirt, coat and tie; shells found at the death scene, two loaded shells found on the seat of the Deskin car, and Deskin's and Arnold's shoes.

Sheriff Lovitt I. Westlake was the first witness of this session to testify. He stated that he had retrieved the Deskin car, a 1930 green Chevrolet sedan, from Clarence Arnold's cabin, 209 Black Street, about 2 a.m. the morning after the murder. He drove the car up to the jail, and Deskin, who was occupying one of the front cells at the time, saw his car and asked, "Who drove my car up here?"

Next, Deputy Tom Marley told about matching the car's tire tracks. He had driven the Deskin car to a sandy place in front of John Railey's house for the purpose of making tire prints in the sand. He submitted a photo of the tracks in the sand, as well as a photo of the car tracks at the scene of the murder that were in the loose dirt there. He said that the tracks in both photos matched. He had also fitted Deskin's shoes in the dusty prints at the murder scene, eight to ten feet from where the body had lain, and he had fitted Arnold's shoes in the dusty prints at the scene by where the dead body was found. He concluded that both men's shoes were a perfect match in the dusty prints at the crime scene.

Alfred Schlecten, local Bozeman photographer, then took the stand and identified the photos of the tire tracks, as well as the photo of the dead body of Kelly lying on a stretcher.

Guy Griffin, the Deskins' neighbor, testified that it was between 4 and 4:30 p.m. when Jim had staggered across the potato patch with the shotgun, asking Griffin to keep the gun for him until he called for it. Mr. and Mrs. George Hoell, he said, were standing near Griffin's pigpen talking to Griffin when Jim appeared with the gun.

George Hoell followed Griffin to the stand. He told the court that when Jim Deskin came over to Griffin's with the gun, he wasn't staggering, and the time was closer to 5 p.m., because he heard the cereal mill whistle sound, as it did every day at that time.

Dr. Frank Cotner, bacteriologist at Montana State College, identified the bloodstains on the Deskin car and on Deskin's and Arnold's shoes and had analyzed the stains, stating they were definitely human blood.

Taking the stand next was Charles Raper, embalmer at the Dokken Funeral Parlor, where the body of Kelly had been taken after being removed from the crime scene. Raper said he arrived at the scene about 10 p.m.-11 p.m. on September 20 and felt the man's body. It was cold, and rigor mortis had already set in. He estimated the time of death to have been somewhere between 4-6 p.m. that evening. Raper described the wound in the back of the victim's neck in detail. Then the bloody coat and shirt of the victim were introduced as evidence.

Floyd Summers, a bellhop at the Bozeman Hotel, testified next. He had gone to the Dokken Funeral Parlor to view the dead body, and it was indeed the body of William Kelly, who had registered at the hotel earlier in the day on the 20th. He said the man was a large, fat man who rolled when he walked, and weighed about 240 pounds and was about five feet ten inches tall. He was approximately 45 years old.

Reverend Hugh Foley, priest of the chapel at Fort Harrison Veterans Hospital, testified that he had seen William Kelly at the hospital there, and he identified the body of the dead man as Kelly.

Deputy Tom Marley was recalled to the witness stand, and he told of finding Deskin's car at the Arnold cabin at 2 a.m. the morning after the shooting. He said two loaded shotgun shells were found in the front seat of the car, as well as a homemade "sap" or billy, made from a piece of rubber hose.

Ward McVey, a local farmer, testified that he had been hired to guard the murder scene from the time the police arrived until 4 p.m. the next day. It was during this time that photographer, Alfred Schlecten, had come and taken photos of the undisturbed location.

Sheriff Westlake took the stand and said that the Deskin car had three Goodyear tires and one Riverside tire, which was on the left rear wheel. He said that the tracks made at the murder scene matched the tracks taken in the sand and were very discernable, due to the odd tire on the left wheel. Westlake said that he had taken the shotgun wadding and pellets that were removed from Kelly's head, along with his coat, shirt and necktie, and delivered them to county attorney, Fred Lay, who traveled by train to Seattle to have them examined by Luke S. May, noted criminologist.

All through the trial that day, Jim Deskin had paid close attention to the testimonies, seeming to be puzzled by some of it, and had at times conferred with his attorneys. He hadn't appeared to be worried too much by the state's case thus far!

The crowd in the courtroom on the third day of the Deskin trial was even greater than any previous day of the present term of court, and seats were filled long before court opened that day. All available standing room, including space between the west wall of the room and the judge's dais, was filled all during the day. There were about 250 people in the room, which was designed to hold only 150. All seats were taken up! It was almost a certainty that Arnold would take the stand today, as the only witness to the crime!

Clarence Arnold was indeed the state's first witness of the day to take the stand. The courtroom was so quiet that, if a pin had been dropped, it would have been heard!

Arnold said that he, James Deskin, and Earl and William Pierce were at the Arnold cabin, located at 209 S. Black, on September 20. About two o'clock, Leland Ping and John Burnett, a Belgrade farmer, arrived at the cabin. They drank two or three inches of a quart of whiskey, and then Burnett offered to buy a jug of beer if somebody would go get it. It was obtained, and they drank that. Then another jug was secured and consumed. Burnett then decided he'd buy a pony (four gallon) keg of beer. Arnold and Ping went to the Park Cigar Store to purchase the keg, where Arnold saw William Kelly, whom he'd known at Fort Harrison Veterans Hospital when they were both patients there. Arnold invited Kelly to come to the cabin and join the men in the beer drinking. Kelly told him that he was broke and couldn't buy any beer. Arnold told him that Burnett was doing the buying, so Kelly agreed to go with the two men.

When they arrived at Arnold's cabin, he introduced Kelly to the rest of the men. After a few rounds, Kelly explained that he was broke and couldn't buy any beer, and James Deskin called Kelly a vile name and told him to pay up. Then Deskin called him the name again, and this time Kelly slapped Deskin's face. After awhile, Kelly and Deskin shook hands and did so several times that afternoon. Everyone thought the two men had become pals and that the earlier altercation had been forgotten.

About 4 p.m., Deskin said that he had to go home and take his wife shopping. Arnold went along, and Jim went into the Deskin house and came back carrying a shotgun. He told Arnold, "The old lady ain't ready yet — let's go shoot some prairie chickens."

Deskin suggested they stop by Arnold's cabin to see if any of the others wanted to go along. Arnold went to the outhouse, and when he came back, Kelly was sitting in the front seat by Jim. Kelly invited Clarence to go along. Arnold climbed into the back seat.

They drove out south of town on Sour Dough Road and turned into Keggie's Lane, and Kelly asked Deskin to stop the car — he wanted to get out for a moment. Arnold said, "Kelly got out on the right hand side, facing almost west, toward the back of the car. Deskin got out on the left side with the shotgun and went around the front of the car to the right side, and, when he was just about at the bumper, he raised the gun, took aim and fired."

Then Arnold said Deskin threw the empty shell out of the gun, stepped around to the left side of the car again and pointed the gun at Clarence, telling him to get out and turn Kelly over. Arnold did just that and got back into the front seat.

Arnold asked Deskin, "My God, Jim, what have you done?" Jim answered, "No S.O.B. is gonna slap me and get by with it!" Arnold told Deskin that Kelly had been his friend. Jim said, "Friend, hell, he ain't the first S.O.B. I've killed, and if you squawk, you'll be next!"

They then drove to Deskin's house, where Arnold discovered he had blood on one of his pant legs. Deskin took a knife and cut it off and told Clarence that his wife, Grace, would cut the other one off for him with the scissors. As Grace was cutting the other pant leg off, she asked Arnold, "What are you tryin' to do — make stagged pants out of these trousers?"

Then, Deskin, Grace and Arnold all drove to town in the Deskin car, went to Ray Eldridge's house, drank some beer, and picked up Earl Pierce. Grace Deskin got groceries and they drove back to the Deskin house, where Jim told Clarence and Earl to take the car back up town. Earl took the car to Arnold's cabin.

After finishing his testimony, Arnold stepped down from the stand, and Earl Pierce, William Pierce, Lee Ping and John Burnett took the stand and backed up Clarence Arnold's testimony.

Jim Deskin's face had turned white for an instant as Arnold had told about the shooting, but during most of the testimony he maintained a poker-masked face.

The last witness for the state was criminologist Luke S. May of Seattle. He testified that he had examined the shotgun, clothing of the deceased man, the 39 pellets and shotgun wadding extracted from the victim's neck, along with the shell found near the dead man's body. He concluded that the shotgun owned by Deskin was indeed the murder weapon.

The state finished its case at 3:38 p.m. The defense produced testimony moments later, starting even without an opening.

The first witness for the defense was Tom Lawrence, embalmer apprentice at the Dokken Funeral Parlor. He testified that the victim, William Kelly, still felt warm when he was brought in to the funeral parlor shortly after midnight.

Then Guy Griffin was called back on the stand, and he reaffirmed that the time he received the gun from Jim was between 4 and 4:15 p.m. on the afternoon of September 20.

Grace Deskin took the stand on her husband's behalf. She contradicted the state's story when she said that Jim and Clarence had come to the house about four o'clock and Arnold asked her to cut off his trouser legs. He told her they were ragged, and he'd tried to cut them off with his knife. She trimmed off the ragged one and then cut the other one to match. She saw no sign of blood on either leg of the trousers.

Clarence Arnold wanted to borrow Jim's shotgun, she said, but she said Jim was pretty drunk and she didn't want him going all over town with it, so she had talked him into taking the gun over to Guy Griffin's. Then they all went up town.

On the way uptown they picked up Ping and Burnett and went to Eldridge's house about 4:20 p.m. and drank some beer.

Then they drove to the business section of town to get groceries. She said the men all got in the car while she was getting the groceries and drove away, and it was some time before they returned. Then they went to the Deskin house, taking the groceries, about 5:20 p.m.

When Grace and Jim got home, they had a fight, and Jim told Clarence and Earl to take the car. Jim stayed home then, until he went to Griffin's to get the children, who had been there since school was out.

When she was cross-examined, Grace said that Jim had knocked her down with a blow in the eyes during their fight.

Ray Eldridge took the witness stand again, verifying that the time Grace said they were at his house that afternoon was correct. The state cross-examined him and reminded him that he'd told police officers earlier when they'd questioned him that he hadn't gotten home from work until after 5:30 p.m. that day. Eldridge said he'd been frightened that day and now, since he was calmer, it had been earlier in the afternoon that he'd been home from work.

The last witness of the day was a young man named Forest Thompson. He said that he knew Kelly, and while driving his girlfriend home on September 20, he had seen William Kelly standing at the corner of Mendenhall and Rouse around 6 p.m. with two other men. Thompson said he stopped the car about 30 feet away because he thought there might be a fight. When it appeared things were going to be okay, he had driven on.

CHAPTER TWENTY-TWO

AT THE BEGINNING of day four of the trial, the state cross-examined Forest Thompson, who told them the day before that he'd seen Kelly alive around 6 p.m. on the day he was murdered. Thompson retracted his story when he saw that his girlfriend, May Thompson (unrelated to Forest), was in the courtroom and would probably testify. He said he guessed he didn't stop at the corner of Mendenhall and Rouse and had just taken his girlfriend on home.

May Thompson took the stand next and said she and Forest Thompson went straight from where he picked her up at a beauty parlor to her home and that they hadn't stopped anywhere along the way.

Testifying in his own behalf, James Deskin told the court his side of the story. It was much the same as his wife's earlier testimony. He stated that he had left the Arnold cabin about four o'clock in the afternoon. Kelly, he said, stayed at the cabin, but Clarence Arnold had driven with him to the Deskin house to pick up Grace and take her uptown to buy groceries.

On the way to Deskin's place, Arnold tried to get Jim to "soak" his shotgun to buy a gallon of whiskey so that Arnold could start bootlegging again. When they got to the house, Grace persuaded him to take the gun over to Guy Griffin's house for him to keep. He said he went to Griffin's just after four o'clock. Grace had trimmed a ragged trouser leg that Arnold had attempted to cut off with a knife, and then she trimmed the other leg to match. They then went to town.

They picked up Burnett and Ping, and all of them went to the Eldridge home about 4:20 p.m. and drank beer.

Later they took Grace to town to get the groceries and had

trouble parking the car, as at first, they'd parked in front of the Baltimore Hotel and a man had come out and told them to move the car. Deskin was out of the car when he noticed his car moving away with Ping driving. Ping parked it in front of Art Nash's house to get it out of the way of the hotel passenger zone.

Then Deskin wanted a drink, so they drove up to the Arnold cabin. Ping and Burnett got out, and Earl Pierce got in the car, and they went back downtown looking for Grace Deskin.

After finding Grace, Arnold took the wheel, and Grace asked him, "Where the hell you been?" She got her groceries and got in the back seat, and they drove back to the Deskin home. Once inside, Grace complained to Jim about being left uptown with the groceries, and she wouldn't shut up about it. Jim said that he told Grace to "Go put your groceries away and shut your mouth!" She then wrapped the sack of groceries around his head, and he hit her and knocked her down and motioned for Arnold to go on and drive the car away.

Grace and Jim made up after their fight, he started a fire, and she prepared some lunch while he went to Griffins' after the kids. When he returned, he had a couple bowls of soup and went to bed. He didn't wake up until the police were at the door at 4 a.m. and took him to the county jail.

Deskin said that he didn't call Kelly a name at the Arnold cabin earlier that day, and that Kelly did not slap his face. He said he had heard Clarence Arnold remark that he wished Kelly would go to sleep so that he could roll him, when he (Deskin) had gone to the outhouse out back of the cabin.

James Deskin testified that Kelly never explained that he was broke because there was no occasion for him to do so. He said the men at the cabin drank most of a quart of whisky, two-gallon jugs and one four-gallon keg of beer. Deskin said that he was pretty drunk when he left there at four o'clock.

Ivan Thew and Ray Eldridge then took the stand and said that Clarence Arnold's reputation for truth-telling was not good.

Thomas Ramey and May Monroe testified that they had been at the Deskin house the night of September 20 and had left about 9:15 p.m., at which time Jim Deskin was in bed asleep.

All day long, and even one hour before the court convened for the day, the courtroom was jammed with curious spectators. Many had to stand and had remained in there from the time the evidence was completed at 2:15 p.m., until 5 p.m., when the attorneys and Judge Berg had finished with their instructions to the jury. The instructions were read to them before the suppertime recess, and the attorneys began their pleas with the opening of the evening session. The largest number of people attended during the pleas, and queues of people were listening, standing on tiptoes outside the courtroom doors, trying to see inside.

Judge Berg told the jury that they could find the defendant guilty of murder in the first degree, which carried a punishment of hanging or life imprisonment at the state prison in Deer Lodge. Or they could decide that Deskin was too drunk to know what he was doing and charge him with second degree murder, which was punishable by a prison term of not less than ten years and not more than 99 years. If the jury should decide to believe the defense's story, they could declare him not guilty and free Deskin.

The jury began deliberating the case at 9:30 p.m. on Saturday night, November 24. They went to bed at midnight without giving any indication as to what verdict they had reached. Fifty people, including Grace and Wilmath, stayed in the courtroom all evening, waiting for the verdict.

Sunday morning, November 25, at 10 a.m., there were only 12 spectators in the courtroom. The jury was ready to announce its verdict.

James Deskin arrived in the room, handcuffed to Sheriff Westlake. He came in smiling and nodded to a few friends and to his wife and mother. The jury filed in and handed the verdict to Judge Berg. The judge handed it to the clerk of the district court, L. E. Hays, who read the verdict. The jury had found the defendant, 36-year-old James Deskin, guilty of murder in the first degree. The punishment was life imprisonment at the state penitentiary at Deer Lodge!

After hearing the verdict read by the clerk, Deskin's face lit up for a second or two, then he turned and smiled to the sheriff and said, "Well, let's go." He was relieved! As Jim and the sheriff got up to leave the courtroom, Wilmath and Grace came forward to embrace him with tears in their eyes. Wilmath's wail could be heard throughout the building!

Wilmath had to take to her bed for several days following the trial. She was tired on the inside, as well as physically, on the outside. She felt so sorry for Jim and Grace and the children!

Grace visited Jim at the jail and told Wilmath that Judge Berg would be passing formal sentencing on December 1, and at that time he'd probably be taken to Deer Lodge.

Wilmath went to the jail to see Jim the day before his appearance before the judge. "Oh, son," she began, "I'm feelin' so bad about this!"

"Mother, try not to get so upset — I'll be okay," he said, trying to comfort her.

"Don't you worry — I intend to get a lawyer workin' for you, and we're gonna do whatever it takes to get you out of there," she promised.

"I know you'll do what you can — that's all any of us can hope for," he said.

"I've been thinkin' — I'll need to go back to St. Paul and move here — see after your family. I think Lonzo could get back on the Northern Pacific again, now that things are lookin' up a little around this part of the country."

"You better talk to Grace first. I don't know what she'll want to do."

"I promise you, Jim — I'll get you out of that place if I have to go all the way to the top — even to the Governor!"

"I know you would if you thought that would work," he said, knowing his mother very well.

Judge Benjamin Berg passed formal judgment on James Deskin for the murder of William Kelly on December 1, 1934. He indicated that the jurors were lenient in giving the defendant a life sentence.

He also said that Deskin "didn't give Kelly a chance for his life." He further stated, "You have no sympathy coming to you — but your wife and family are deserving of deepest sympathy because of your committing the most heinous crime that man can do. Your defense did all they could for you in the face of such strong evidence, while the counsel for the state was not bloodthirsty in their prosecution."

Jim was taken immediately to Deer Lodge to start serving his sentence.

After Jim left for the prison, Wilmath had a talk with Grace.

"What're you thinkin' of doin' now, Grace, and how will you

provide for Lee and Peggy?"

"I have family in Three Forks. I was thinkin' of tryin' to sell the ranch and go up there and take the children. One of my brothers says they need help at a laundry where he works. I'll have to get a job somewhere!"

"I'd like to go back to St. Paul right away. I have to talk to Lonzo, but I think that he may be able to get back on the Northern Pacific. I've always liked it here around Bozeman — the Bridger Mountains and all. I think we could buy this place and take over your note. I could fix it up some, have a garden, raise some potatoes, maybe have a milk cow and some chickens. Why don't you stay here until I can get things rounded up in St. Paul? You can visit Jim while I'm in Minnesota — we've got to keep that boy's spirits up — we're all he's got! I'm gonna do everything I can to get him outta there!"

"I wish you could, but that won't be easy! He may never get out!"

"Don't even think that way, girl. I refuse to think he's gonna have to spend the rest of his life in prison!"

Wilmath traveled to St. Paul, and Lonzo told her that while she was in Montana he had gone to the railroad's headquarters which were located there in town, and he had been hired once again by the Northern Pacific and would be working out of Livingston. He also informed "the Mrs." that he had already had an offer from his niece and her husband to purchase the diner.

The Garrens returned to Montana, Lonzo going on to Livingston while Wilmath went to Bozeman. They were prepared to buy the ranch! Jim had been at the prison about a month. Grace had gone to Deer Lodge and talked to him about selling the farm to his mother and stepfather, and he thought that it was a good idea. That way, Grace would be out from under the thousand-dollar debt on the place.

Grace went to the lawyer's office to sign the deed over to the Garrens. Then they had to take the attorney with them to Deer Lodge and have Jim sign the papers as well.

It was winter, and Peggy was still in school. Wilmath told Grace to go on to Three Forks and begin her new job and she'd take care of the children. Lonzo was working in Livingston during the week, but he came back home to Bozeman to the roundhouse each Friday night on the train. Lonzo purchased a 1930

Model A Ford pickup truck so that Wilmath would have transportation with him gone all week.

Spring came to Bozeman, but the temperatures were still chilly. Wilmath made regular visits to the prison to see Jim, taking him cake, pie, fried chicken and cigarettes. Jim had been working in the workshop at the penitentiary, and he'd made a leather belt for his mother.

Deer Lodge was located in Powell County, and it was 123 miles from Bozeman. Sometimes Wilmath drove there in the pickup, but she had ridden the train in the winter months.

As one approached the city, the enormous red brick 1896 cell house with rounded towers loomed over Deer Lodge. The building was no longer in use, as a more modern facility had been built in 1912. The depression of 1893 left the state without funds for improvements to the prison. Warden Frank Conley had solicited convict labor for expanding the prison. Almost all the structures on the grounds had been built by inmates.

The Administration Building was only three years old. Wilmath had to enter this facility and check in with office personnel before visiting Jim. The building was the hub of security and the heart of prison operations. Offices, visiting rooms, a library, classrooms and a mailroom and infirmary were on the main floor.

The visiting room for medium-minimum security was located to the left of the doorway of the building. The bottom of the partition was solid, preventing the passing of contraband. The top was wire mesh screening. It was here that Jim appeared for his visit with his mother.

"Mother, what do you hear from Grace?" he asked one spring day. "She hasn't written much, and I haven't seen her for a while."

"Well, son, she writes to the children. She's workin' and that's about all she says, outside of sayin' she misses them. They're doin' fine out there with me. I got them feedin' the chickens and hoein' the garden. We pick Lonzo up every Friday at the roundhouse. As soon as they get in school, I'm getting you a lawyer, and we're gonna see about getting you outta here!"

"You don't give up, do you, Mother?"

"No, son — you don't belong in here, and I'll see to it that you get out!"

The visit was soon at an end, and as Wilmath left the building, she looked around at the cell house, which was built in 1912. Each cell had running water, flush toilets and good ventilation. She noticed that the new Tag Plant and Hospital Building would soon be finished. It would house the infirmary, surgical hospital, dental laboratory, psychiatric ward and doctor's office. At the west end of the building, the tag plant contained the auto license plate factory. Across the yard was the W.A. Clark Theater, where a variety of events were held for the convicts, including boxing, movies, plays and religious services. She'd be glad when Jim was out of here and she no longer had to view these sights!

In mid-summer, Jim got a surprise — Grace had written that she wanted a divorce. After all, what chance did their marriage have if he was going to spend the rest of his life in prison? She explained that she was a young woman with her whole life ahead of her.

When Wilmath heard of Grace's request, she decided to try and get custody of Peggy and Lee. She went to see James Murrow, Jr., one of the Bozeman attorneys that had represented Jim during the trial and had him write a letter to Grace stating her intentions. Grace had engaged an attorney at Three Forks, and he'd written Wilmath's attorney stating that the children needed to reside with their mother. Wilmath could see that Grace would not give up custody of the children without a fight! She decided not to pursue the matter any further.

In the fall of 1935 Peggy and Lee went to stay with their mother at Three Forks and started school there. They promised to write their grandmother, but Wilmath knew she would be lonely without them.

Tump was still living at the Lawson farm just outside of Bozeman. Lonzo thought that it would be a good idea if Tump came to the ranch to live, so that his wife would have some help during the week while he was gone. The old uncle could live in one of the outbuildings. The Garrens would provide for him in return. Tump liked the idea of living with family once again, and the only request he had made when he moved was that of bringing his dog, Mutt, along to the ranch.

With Tump around the place, Wilmath had more free time to work on Jim's case. She contacted G.F. Briggs, who was known to be one of the best criminal lawyers in the state. He agreed to see her every month when he came to the Murrow Law Office in

Bozeman. His fees were fairly high, but Wilmath had faith that he would be worth every penny. Lonzo gave her his paycheck every week, only keeping a few dollars for himself to carry him through the next week of work. Wilmath and Tump raised chickens and vegetables and sold them to the merchants and restaurants in town.

When she met with Briggs in December of that year, he informed her that he would compose a letter to the Governor in Helena, requesting that he set an appointment with Wilmath to discuss Jim's incarceration. He told her that the situation in Helena was not the best. Governor Frank Cooney had died while in office that year of heart failure, and the president pro-tem of the senate, W. Elmer Holt, of Miles City, was acting governor until the election could be held in 1937.

For Wilmath1936 was to be a busy year. One Friday when she went to the roundhouse to bring Lonzo home for the weekend, he had something furry in his arms. It was a small German Shepherd puppy. He explained that the pup had been dumped near one of the train depots, and it would have frozen to death in the cold winter temperatures if he hadn't taken the little dog with him.

When they arrived at the ranch, Mutt and the new dog became instant pals. Since it was a German Shepherd, Lonzo named him Fritz. He would be a good watchdog for Wilmath, and he turned out to be just that! Sometimes he would bark and wake her in the middle of the night, and she'd get the old shotgun out from behind the kitchen door, certain that there was something or someone outside. The only intruders that she had encountered were skunks and possums.

Wilmath took Fritz, who was growing larger each week, to the roundhouse on Fridays, and as soon as Lonzo's train pulled in, Fritz bounded out of the truck and headed for the exact car Lonzo would be disembarking from. Then he walked alongside the tall man, jumping into the back of the pickup as Lonzo opened the passenger door and got in the truck.

In the spring of that year, Wilmath received a letter from Grace, telling her that she'd remarried. Wilmath had written back, asking if Lee and Peggy could spend the summer at the ranch.

Late in May the two Deskin children arrived in Bozeman and

told their grandmother that they didn't like their new stepfather. Wilmath took them to Deer Lodge to visit Jim, who was overjoyed to see them. They spent the summer playing with Mutt and Fritz, helping in the garden and playing in the stream. Wilmath had Tump, with Guy Griffin's help, build a wooden footbridge over the shallow stream that separated the pasture from the barn, so that the cow could get to the barn. Lee learned to milk the cow with old Tump's help. Occasionally he and Peggy would catch trout in the stream, and Wilmath would have a fish fry on the weekends when Lonzo was home. She'd invite the Griffins over, and it was an enjoyable time.

"You sure do know how to cook, Mrs. Garren," the Griffin's son, Ted, told her after the fish fry.

Wilmath was thankful to have the Griffins for neighbors. Guy had stood by Jim all through the trial to the best of his ability. She and Lonzo decided to deed a small parcel of land that adjoined the Griffin property to them, thus paring the Garren property down to exactly five acres.

In the late summer of 1936, Lottie's son, Ernest, was in the CCC near Yellowstone. Ernest was special to Wilmath because he had been her first grandchild. President Franklin Roosevelt had gained congressional approval for a project called the Civilian Conservation Corps. The CCC gave temporary employment to 250,000 unmarried men between the ages of 18 and 25, 25,000 World War I Veterans, and 25,000 experienced woodsmen. Most of the men received $30 a month, $25 of which were sent to their families. They were given board and lodging in camp and put to work on useful projects in the national forests.

Ernest had gotten out of high school, worked for various farmers in northeastern Missouri a while, and then went to the CCC. The Missouri unit was taken to Salt Lake City, Utah, to work on a golf course there. Ernest was sent to a Caterpillar school in Nevada. He worked in Utah about a month and then was transferred to Yellowstone Park. In order to get out of the CCC, the men had to have employment somewhere.

Wilmath wrote to Ernest and told him he could get a job at a warehouse in Bozeman and stay at the ranch with her while he worked there. He was 21 years old, and a big handsome man! The job at the warehouse lasted 12 days. Then Ernest helped Wilmath around the ranch. She also wanted him to drive her to

Helena to see the Governor when she got an appointment and also to Deer Lodge to see Jim.

In August, Mr. Briggs called Wilmath and told her he had set up an appointment with Governor Elmer Holt to discuss Jim's case. Peggy and Lee were at the ranch, but they would be returning to Three Forks in September to start school.

One day in August before her appointment with the Governor, Ernest drove his grandmother to Deer Lodge to see Jim. He hadn't seen his uncle in over four years. When Jim saw Ernest, he was glad to see his big strapping nephew.

"I didn't know you were in our neck of the woods, Ernest," Jim said, glad to see his relative.

"Grandma got me out of the CCC — I've been up at the ranch a few weeks. Jim, I haven't forgotten that time you, Grace and the kids all came to Knox City in that rainstorm and we swam across the creek to get to town because you were out of cigarettes."

"That's right — I'm sure glad we made that trip now!"

Ernest and Jim visited a while; then Wilmath said to her son, "Jim, I have an appointment to meet with the Governor in Helena in a week to talk to him about your case. I'm going to ask him to work on a pardon for you! Mr. Briggs thinks we might be able to get one in the works. He has no idea how long it'll take, but whatever time it takes is what it will take!"

A week later, dressed in her finest hat and sequined dress, Wilmath had Ernest drive her to Helena to see the Governor. On the way there, Ernest asked his grandmother if she was nervous about speaking with Governor Holt.

"Land sakes, no," she replied in answer to his question. "He's just a man like all other men! The most important thing I'm thinkin' about is getting my Jim out of prison, and this is the only way I know to get the job done!"

Ernest pulled the pickup into the parking lot and waited in the truck while he watched Wilmath, shoulders back, walk up the sidewalk, then up a flight of steps to the door of the state capitol. He would always say one thing for his grandma — she had more guts than any woman he had ever known!

Governor Holt made no promises to Wilmath, but agreed to look into the matter. After she had left his office, the Governor thought, that is one strong and courageous woman! Ernest was curious about his grandmother's visit with the head of the state, but she didn't give him many details.

She had decided not to mention much about Jim's incarceration to her two daughters and their families back in Missouri. All they had been told at the time of Jim's trial was that there had been some type of hunting accident while Jim and some other men were out shooting prairie chickens, and a man had been accidentally shot. She asked Ernest not to discuss Jim's situation with any of the folks back home.

Ernest and the Deskin children knew that their grandma was very superstitious. She always carried a rabbit's foot in her beaded purse. Most of the time she carried her money in a tobacco pouch, which she fastened to the inside of her top undergarments. This was due to her mistrust of banks, since they'd had failures in the past. Some superstitions affected her daily life. She never swept the floor after dark and would go miles out of her way to avoid crossing the path of a black cat. She'd also have certain "feelings" about things that were about to happen.

Wilmath didn't want Seba to know the gruesome details of Jim's imprisonment. She'd heard little from him and had taken the letters he'd sent Jim up to the prison when she went. Seba had written a postcard to Wilmath recently, telling her that he had gone to Knox City to visit Lottie and had seen Wilmath's new grandchild, Donald, who was a year old. It was Lottie's eighth child!

She'd only mentioned Seba to Lee and Peggy once in a roundabout way. Peggy had asked Grandma about her relatives back in Missouri, and Wilmath had told her little. She especially didn't want the two Deskin grandchildren to know about all of her previous marriages. The only thing she told Peggy in answer to her question was that she had loved someone very dearly and couldn't ever have him! The other thing she told her was that both her aunts in Missouri were tied down with lots of children, especially Lottie!

Lonzo tried to talk Ernest into becoming a boxer. The big man had the build for it, but Ernest wasn't interested. He could tell that Lonzo was a died-in-the-wool boxing fan. Lonzo told him about the famous fight in Shelby that he'd attended in 1923, when Jack Dempsey had beat Tommy Gibbons. Now America's interest had turned to Joe Louis, the black boxer from Detroit. In

1935 he had beat Primo Carnera and Max Baer, both former heavyweight champions. He'd had 27 victories, 23 knockouts, and no losses. In June of 1936, at Yankee Stadium, he had fought Max Schmeling, and it had been Louis' first loss in 28 professional fights. Lonzo told Ernest that he had a bet on with some of the fellows he worked with, that in 1937 the boxer would be a winner!

CHAPTER TWENTY-THREE

ONE EVENING in October 1936, Ernest had gone to the outhouse in back of his grandma's house and was walking along beside the front of the house. He'd gotten as far as the porch, when he looked toward Old Baldy and the Bridger Mountains. Grandma had told him that the peak was supposed to be "an indicator of happenings." It was close to seven o'clock and dark outside when Ernest noticed an odd radiation that seemed to "light up" Old Baldy. He couldn't believe it! What was going on! He ran into the house.

"Grandma," he shouted, "come out on the porch quick — Old Baldy's lit up!" Wilmath followed her grandson out on the porch. Ernest felt foolish — Old Baldy was shrouded in total darkness.

"I know what I saw, Grandma — it really was lit up!"

"I'm not doubtin' you, Ernest. I told you there was somethin' mysterious about that mountain — that was a sign of somethin'." As he went into the kitchen, he noticed that the hands on the clock on the cook stove were pointing precisely at seven o'clock.

The following morning the Garrens' phone rang. Wilmath answered it — it was Lottie!

"Mamma," she said, "somethin' terrible happened last night — Uncle C.B. was killed in a car accident down at Macon about eight o'clock last night!" Wilmath handed the receiver to Ernest, her body starting to sway. Ernest hung up the phone and caught his grandmother as she had almost fainted right there on the floor!

He carried her to her bed, which was in one corner of the kitchen. She had fixed up the one bedroom in the house for Ernest to stay in while he was there. He was currently fanning her with a magazine that was lying close by, as she lay on the bed with her eyes closed. After a while she opened her eyes, looked around, then closed them again.

Ernest was shaking her and demanding, "What's wrong, Grandma — what happened?"

A flood of tears poured from her eyes, streaming down her face, and she sobbed hysterically, "Seba got killed last night! He's gone!" Then she turned on her side, her back to him, and cried until Ernest thought she would never stop. He heard her mutter something about Old Baldy being a sign, and then her lips shut tightly and she lay there the rest of the day in silent mourning.

Wilmath stayed in bed all of the next day and sent Ernest into town for some medicine for a massive throbbing headache. When he returned, she took her medicine and then told him that he needed to go back to Macon County and attend his uncle's funeral.

"I've been thinkin', Ernest. You must catch the next train out of Bozeman and go to Missouri to your uncle's funeral. You should get there in plenty of time, as they'll have to wait for Charley to get there from Texas and Ren will be coming from California. I can't go — you must go in my place!"

Ernest didn't understand why his grandmother was so adamant about this, but he thought it was time he should be getting back to northeastern Missouri anyway. He agreed to take the first train he could find going out of Bozeman that day, and he promised Wilmath faithfully that he would attend the funeral and write to her afterward.

Several weeks later Ernest wrote her that he had attended the funeral at Mt. Tabor Church near Atlanta and the burial there following the service. He had also written that John's boy, Roy, had been driving the car, and another car had hit the Dennis vehicle on the passenger side, causing Seba's instant death. Roy had survived but was in the hospital.

By the middle of 1937, Wilmath still hadn't recovered from Seba's death. She'd gone to the prison for her visit with Jim soon after the tragedy and told him of Seba's accident and demise, but she would never let him know that he had just lost his real father! What good would it do now!

She would spend her time now concentrating on freeing Jim. A new governor had been elected this year — Roy Ayres, a Democrat and former Fergus County rancher. She would talk to Mr. Briggs and see if she could get an appointment with the new official.

Two weeks later she was in Briggs' office. He told her that this was a bad time to contact the Governor because of the upheaval in the Democratic Party. Senator B.K. Wheeler, who was one of Montana's most influential political figures, had broken relations with President Franklin Roosevelt over the President's attempt to "pack" the Supreme Court with friendly judges. Many Republicans and the more conservative Democrats had agreed with Wheeler's actions. Representative Jerry O'Connell was encouraged by the President to fight to defeat Wheeler and his colleagues. The left wing of the Democratic Party had risen up in rebellion against Wheeler and Governor Ayres. Thus, chaos was reigning in Helena.

Briggs assured Wilmath he'd do what he could regarding her visit to the capitol.

She continued to visit Jim at Deer Lodge. He was looking well and behaving at the prison. She told him that his good record at the facility should help in obtaining a pardon.

During the summer of 1937, Eva Dent, Lottie's daughter, came to spend the summer with her grandma. Peggy and Lee were there also. All three grandchildren, along with Tump, tended the garden and did the chores. Eva rode to Deer Lodge to the prison with them whenever they visited Jim. Wilmath had wallpapered the walls of one of the sheds out back of the house, and Eva slept there on a cot. Paul Garren, Lonzo's brother, was visiting from Fletcher, North Carolina, and he occupied the one bedroom in the house.

In 1938 Lonzo and Wilmath decided to tear down the old house they were living in and build a new log house on the property. Several neighbors helped Lonzo and Tump cut logs, and the four-room house was finally finished in the summer. The outbuildings were torn down, as some had almost fallen down on their own.

There had been no news about obtaining the appointment with the present governor. Mr. Briggs was still working to arrange a meeting with him for Wilmath. Senator Wheeler had managed to get O'Connell defeated by a Republican. The state government was still embroiled in a turmoil.

Lonzo wanted to go to North Carolina to visit his mother, Delia, and his brothers and sisters in Fletcher, North Carolina, in the summer of 1939. His brother, Alvin, had passed away, and Lonzo had gone down alone to attend the funeral, as Wilmath was busy with the grandchildren and running the farm when he died. "The Mrs." had never met Lonzo's family. He thought it would be good for her to get away for a while. They boarded the train at Bozeman and headed for North Carolina after stopping several places along the way.

They stopped at St. Paul to see relatives and friends. Rex Garren had passed away, but his daughter was still running the diner. Wilmath and Lonzo saw several of their old customers one day while they were visiting at the eating establishment.

Buffalo, New York, was their next destination. It was here that they crossed into Canada to view the breathtaking Niagara Falls. The place was a popular "honeymoon mecca." Wilmath had never had a honeymoon, even though she'd been married several times. They went back over to the United States side then, to view the Bridal Veil Falls.

Lonzo knew that his wife had always loved amusement parks, so they rode the train from Brooklyn to Coney Island. They ate foot-long hot dogs and cotton candy. He and Wilmath even rode the ferris wheel and the roller coaster! Lonzo thought he saw a sparkle in his wife's eyes that he hadn't seen in them for some time.

They traveled southwest to the western part of North Carolina to Asheville, and on south of there to the small town of Fletcher. Wilmath liked Lonzo's mother, Delia, who was quite elderly. But she had been appalled at the lifestyle of these folks!

Soon after they had arrived, Wilmath asked Delia if she had a washboard so that she might do some laundry. Sending her daughter-in-law out to the back porch of the small meager house, Wilmath hardly recognized the washboard. It was only made of a few crude horizontal sticks that were nailed to some vertical sticks that served as a frame! She managed to wash out a few of their things.

On the way back from North Carolina, they stopped at South Bend, Indiana, to visit with Earl and Laura Dennis and daughters, Regina and Adel. Earl had a job working on the assembly line at the Studebaker automobile factory there.

When they got to Missouri, they came through Knox City on the "Q" and were met by Clyde Dent, who took the Garrens out to the farm southwest of town. Wilmath hadn't seen Lottie's last child, Donald, who was four years old by now!

At Kansas City, they were met at Union Station by Orville Curry. Ollie was happy to see her mother and stepfather. Wilmath became acquainted with little Donna, Ollie's sixth child! She told Ollie that she thought it was high time that she and Lottie quit having babies.

In the gubernatorial election of 1940, Montana liberal Democrats set out to defeat the more conservative Democrats, especially Senator Wheeler and Governor Roy Ayers. Ayers lost the election to Republican Sam C. Ford. However, Wheeler won a fourth senate term.

Wilmath spent the year 1940 working with G.F. Briggs, trying to secure an appointment with Governor Ford. By early 1941 she decided to try another approach. She went to Mr. Briggs' office and insisted that he place a call to the state capitol. She would try to speak to the Governor over the phone if nothing else. Briggs placed the call, which was answered by Walter P. Coombs, assistant secretary to the Governor.

Taking the phone in hand, Wilmath got right to the point with her request. "Mr. Coombs, I am the mother of James Deskin, who is serving a life sentence at the state prison. I would like to arrange a meeting with Governor Ford this week."

The secretary replied, "Yes, Mrs. Garren, we have numerous letters from Mr. Briggs pertaining to your request to see Governor Ford. I'm afraid that I cannot make an appointment until I have conferred with the Governor. I will write you as soon as I have spoken with him."

Several days later a letter came in the mail from Walter Coombs. It read:

"Dear Mrs. Garren,

Reference is made to our telephone conversation in which you asked for an appointment this week with the Governor.

I have taken the matter up with Governor Ford, and he has asked me to advise you that, due to the great press of important state business, he will be unable to see you at all this week. He has board meetings and committee hearings scheduled for the entire period, and regrets exceed-

ingly that he knows of no time when he will be available.
Cordially yours,
Walter P. Coombs, Assistant Secretary

Wilmath was undaunted by the letter which was a refusal of her request. She asked Briggs to continue to work toward the endeavor.

In the spring of 1942, G.F. Briggs called Wilmath and told her that he had received a letter from Walter Coombs, and that Governor Ford would be able to see her on April 3.

She decided to ride to Helena on the train. She wanted to be rested and well groomed for her appearance before Governor Sam C. "Model T" Ford. On April 3 she was wearing a hat from one of Bozeman's finest shops, and her dress was made of the best material one could buy west of the Mississippi. She was not only stylish, but she was elegant and distinguished-looking for a lady of 60.

She took a cab to the state capitol upon arriving at the train station in Helena. Walking into the office of the Governor, she was a sight to behold! Governor Ford was himself an attractive man, with a round face that sported wire-rimmed glasses.

Wilmath, whose manners were impeccable, extended a gloved hand to the Governor. "How do you do, Governor," she said gracefully. "I am Wilmath Garren, mother of James Deskin, who currently is being held at the Deer Lodge Prison."

"Yes, Mrs. Garren, I've been expecting you. Won't you please be seated here in front of my desk?" he asked as he pointed to a nearby chair. Once she was seated, the Governor continued. "Mr. Coombs, my secretary, has given me several letters from your attorney, Mr. Briggs, requesting that I consider a pardon for your son."

Sam Ford was looking at a thick file of papers containing the prison record of James Deskin. "I need to make sure I have these facts straight before I submit them to the State Board of Pardons." He was shuffling through the myriad of papers as he was speaking. "I understand that your son has been a model prisoner while incarcerated at Deer Lodge and has earned a place of trust there. Is that correct, Mrs. Garren?"

"Yes sir, it is."

"It states here that James has two children who are in great need and are not receiving proper care. Is this true?"

“Yes, it most certainly is!”

“Mrs. Garren, I am going to personally write a letter to the State Board of Pardons stating these facts. In addition, I am going to tell them that the warden at the prison has no objection to your son receiving clemency, and the county attorney and the judge who sentenced him share this same view. I have papers here stating these facts, as well. I will first commute the sentence to 20 years, and then I will write the Board and recommend that a parole be granted to your son.”

Wilmath could hardly believe her ears! She wanted to jump for joy, but a lady would not behave that way, and she WAS a lady! Aloud, she said, “Thank you kindly, Governor.”

“Now, I must tell you — I think that the Board will honor my requests, but we shall have to wait until I get an official answer from them. I will write you as soon as I receive their answer. The matter may take a month or two.” Then the Governor rose from his chair, indicating that the business between them had terminated.

Wilmath stood up, tall and straight, extended her hand once again, and said, “I'm very grateful to you, Governor Ford. Thank you once again!”

He shook her hand and replied, “My pleasure!”

Wilmath went home that day feeling better than she had in years! She wished Seba had been by her side to share this victorious feeling! She had freed their son!

She related the news to Lonzo on Friday afternoon when she picked him up at the roundhouse. Lonzo hadn't seen her this happy in a long, long time. A tremendous burden, he knew, had been lifted from her shoulders!

On June 3, Wilmath went into town to the post office to get her mail. There was a letter from Walter Coombs. It read:

Dear Mrs. Garren:

This is to advise you that Governor Sam C. Ford has recommended that a parole be granted to your son, James Deskin.

The State Board of Pardons will consider this recommendation and if favorable action is taken, your son will be released in about one month.

Sincerely yours,
Walter P. Coombs, Assistant Secretary

Wilmath went to Deer Lodge the next day to tell Jim the news. As she waited for him to appear in the visitors' area, she could hardly contain her excitement! He finally came into the room, grinning from ear to ear. He'd already been notified of the news by the warden.

"Oh, Jim," Wilmath started to cry, "you are finally going to be free!"

"Yes, Mother, it is wonderful news. The warden called me into his office and told me a few days ago. He also notified Grace and the children. And guess what — Grace was up here yesterday. Mother, she wants to get a divorce and wants to marry me again and resume our life with the kids as a family."

Wilmath knew Grace's second marriage wasn't working out, so she wasn't surprised that she wanted a divorce. She was surprised, however, that Grace had moved so fast once she had heard Jim was being pardoned. Aloud, she said, "Son, do you want to marry her again?"

"I know she thought I'd never get out of here, or she wouldn't have divorced me in the first place," he explained. "She told me that the children have never been happy with their stepfather. She said her marriage was in bad shape long ago with this man. We talked it over, and we think it is best for the kids."

"Well, Jim, you know I just want the rest of your life to be happy!"

"I've been told that there is some rule that I have to live in another state when I am released."

"Then, you won't be able to live back on the ranch when you're released — where will you go?"

"I've heard there is a factory in Idaho that makes paper products. They hire a lot of ex-cons. I am going to apply for a job there."

"I just thought of somethin' — you could be released in time for your 44th birthday on the tenth!"

"Yes," he laughed, "I'd thought of that — we'll have to have a big party or some kind of celebration!"

July 5, 1942, Jim called his mother from Deer Lodge and told her that he would be leaving the next day on the train for Bozeman. He wanted Wilmath to meet him at the train station. Grace and the children would be driving to Bozeman later that day and wanted to come to the ranch. His mother assured him that she would be at the station and she'd have a big meal prepared for him, Grace and her grandchildren.

On the afternoon of July 6, James Deskin got off the train a free man! Wilmath greeted him with a big hug, and then they were heading north, going toward the ranch. She could hardly take her eyes off the boy the rest of the day!

Just before dark, Grace, Peggy and Lee arrived. Wilmath had supper ready, and they all sat around the table enjoying the fellowship. Old Tump shuffled in after the meal was over and grasped Jim's hand and smiled at him. Jim patted the old man on the back.

"Tump's not too well, is he?" Jim noticed.

"No, he's getting up there — getting slower all the time."

Grace told Wilmath that she had filed for a divorce and would be moving back to Bozeman soon. She and Jim wanted to go to the courthouse and be married quietly by the judge. Wilmath thought that was probably best, under the circumstances.

The next day was Friday, and they picked Lonzo up at the roundhouse. Jim went along, and Lonzo hurried to the truck, anxious to welcome his stepson back home.

After supper Wilmath said, "Lonzo, Jim is moving to Boise, Idaho, after he and Grace get married. He applied for a job in a paper factory, and they are going to hire him. I always thought he'd be livin' back here at the ranch when he got out, but that isn't gonna happen!"

"I've been thinkin' for some time that maybe we ought to move into town. There's a lot of stuff here for you to care for during the week while I'm gone. And Tump's getting old and feeble and can't do much any more," Lonzo answered.

"That's probably a good idea. What will you do with Tump though?" asked Jim.

"Poor old fellow doesn't have a dime to his name. If I was younger, I'd take him with us and take care of him," Wilmath offered.

"Mother, you're too old to try to do that now," Jim told her.

Lonzo had been thinking. "Maybe he should just go to the County Poor Farm here in Bozeman to live. They'll take care of him."

"That's a thought, but I hate to see him have to go there," Wilmath said sadly.

"Well, Mother, if that's the best thing to do, then there's no other choice," Jim said.

Two months later Jim and Grace were married at the courthouse in Bozeman by a judge, with only Lee and Peggy in attendance. Wilmath had a small reception at the ranch, inviting the Griffins and Grace's relatives. Then she told Jim to look out the window and on out toward the driveway. Lonzo had driven up in a new black 1942 Chevrolet sedan.

"My goodness!" exclaimed Jim. "Did you and Lonzo get a new car?"

"No, son, that's your car — we bought it for you as a going away present, as well as a belated birthday present."

"Oh, Mother, I can't believe it — I've got my freedom, my wife and kids back, and now a new car!" Jim hurried out the door to look the car over from front to back and side to side. Grace and the kids followed. Wilmath stood there watching all the happy smiling faces that were going out the door.

Three days later, James Deskin and family left Bozeman and headed for Boise, Idaho, in the new car. He also had a new job and a brand new life! Relief swept over Wilmath!

Lonzo wanted to sell the ranch before winter, so they put the place up for sale. They also went into town and found a rental house that needed work, but Wilmath enjoyed doing that — it would occupy her time since she would be alone during the week.

November 1942, the ranch was sold, and the Garrens would be in town before wintertime. Wilmath cleaned and decorated the house. Lonzo bought a 1938 Chevrolet sedan. They wouldn't need a pickup now that they lived in town. Wilmath would need a car, as he would still be out of town all week working.

Tump had gone to live at the County Home in Bozeman, which was a two-story brick building on Durston Road. Wilmath could drop in and check on him from time to time. He didn't seem to mind going to live there.

Several months later the director at the Home called her and told her that her old uncle had died. Wilmath decided to sign a paper, donating his body to the Biology Department at Bozeman College. The corpse would be used for experimental purposes by science students. She was sure that poor old Tump wouldn't have minded that!

CHAPTER TWENTY-FOUR

DURING THE NEXT FEW YEARS Wilmath's health slowly began to deteriorate. Lonzo was thinking of retiring from the Northern Pacific Railroad. While they still had access to unlimited train travel due to his job, Wilmath wanted to visit Jim and Grace and her two daughters.

The Jim Deskins had only stayed in Boise, Idaho, about a year. Then they had moved to Salem, Oregon. Jim had gone there once with the warden while still in prison. He had admired the town and thought it would be a nice place to live. He enjoyed the countryside, which was dotted with tall pine trees. Grace had gotten a job in a restaurant in Salem. Jim had gotten a job at a sawmill there. Wilmath and Lonzo were glad to see them living well and happy in Oregon.

The Garrens went to Independence to visit Ollie, Orville and their children. Ollie was working at Lake City, an arsenal that manufactured ammunition. She had started working there in 1942, right after World War II had broken out. Orville was still working at the oil refinery. Four of their children were grown and married. Only Delores and Donna were living at home now.

Lonzo and Wilmath traveled to South Bend, Indiana, to see Lottie and her family. They also visited Earl and Laura Dennis while they were there. Clyde and Lottie had rented out the farm in Knox City, and in 1943 had headed for South Bend. They had trouble earning a living on the northeastern Missouri farm, and Earl had told them there was work in Indiana. Clyde obtained a job working on the railroad, and Lottie was a cook at Smith's Cafeteria, located in the downtown area. Their four youngest boys — C.W., Robert, James and Donald, went to Indiana with their parents. Ernest, who was married, was living in South Bend as well — working at the Studebaker Corporation. The three Dent girls were married and living on farms in northeastern Missouri.

On the way back from South Bend, Lonzo and Wilmath stopped in Missouri to visit the three granddaughters. They went to Macon to visit Victor and his fourth wife, Paula, who lived in a small house by the railroad tracks. On down the street lived Seba's son, Olin, who had taken over his dad's watch repair business. John Dennis had been living in another house close to Vic's and Olin's, and he had passed away in 1943.

The Garrens stopped at the repair shop to visit with Olin Dennis. Wilmath knew he had no idea that she had loved his father or that she always would! He told his Aunt Wilmath, when she had inquired about his sister, Lula May, that she had shortened her name to Maise Dennis and was already becoming successful as an apparel buyer for a famous department store in Dallas.

Wilmath asked Victor if she and Lonzo could borrow his car to drive up to La Plata. She wanted to visit the city cemetery once more where Paulina, Pete and Orena were buried. They drove to the old section of the cemetery where the lone monument stood with the three Dennis names engraved on its front and two sides. Then they drove out to the old farm northeast of La Plata. The house had almost fallen in, and the current owners were using the place solely for farming the ground. Here was the place Wilmath had called home from the time she was two years old.

Daniel Dennis had been transferred to the infirmary in Shelbyville. They stopped by briefly to see Dan, who was the smallest of the Dennis brothers and now was aging. Wilmath had often wondered if he had really suffered the mental problems due to the accident at the well, or if he had simply inherited the illness. Martha Penrod had fallen victim to a nervous condition in her later years.

When they returned to Macon, Vic told them that Charley Dennis was living in Texas and Ren was living in Vacaville, California. As they boarded the Wabash at Macon, Wilmath was thinking that the members of the two Dennis families were rapidly dwindling. Soon, few would be left.

They returned to Bozeman, and Lonzo worked on the railroad one more year. They had moved to five or six different houses in town during that year. Lonzo would laugh and tell people that while he was out all week working, he never knew where "home" would be when he got back into town at end of the week. Wilmath enjoyed fixing up the houses, and when she had accomplished all she could do at one house, she'd move to another rental house and begin to work on it. Sometimes he'd get home and find out they didn't live at the same house he'd left at the beginning of the work week.

Lonzo retired the next year, and they bought a house at 621 North Rouse Street. The Garrens sat on their porch in good weather, visiting with neighbors and friends, inviting some of them in to eat meals with "the two best cooks in town," as those who had partaken of couple's culinary skills had said of them.

In the latter part of September 1949, Wilmath suffered a stroke at her home. She was taken to Deaconess Hospital. The doctors spoke with Lonzo and told him that she was badly affected by the stroke and was partially paralyzed. She was barely able to speak.

Lonzo went into the sterile hospital room and saw his wife lying on the bed, her eyes halfway closed. He slipped quietly into a chair and sat by her bed. He reached for her hand and sat there holding it, saying nothing for some time. Then he stood up and knelt over the bed, speaking directly to his wife.

"Wilmath," he said softly, "can you hear me — it's Lonzo." Her eyes opened wide, and she looked at her husband and nodded her head slightly. Then he saw her trying to move her lips, but no sound came out. He didn't encourage her to talk. He told her he would be back the next day to see her.

A week after suffering the stroke, she could communicate a little better. She was unable to get out of bed, and the paralysis remained in most of the affected parts of her body. Lonzo came to visit and was pleased that she had recognized him and was more alert. When he got ready to leave that day, he asked her if she needed him to bring her anything from the house. She nodded her head. He leaned over her and she said the words— Bible, nightgowns, talcum powder. He knew the talc always sat on their dresser, but he had to ask her where to find the Bible and gowns. She told him that they were in the middle drawer of their chest.

He arrived the next day with the items she'd requested. She asked him to place them on a table next to the bed. She uttered the words "thank you."

The second week in October, she was able to talk better, but still wasn't out of bed. The doctor told Lonzo that, while she seemed to be trying to rally, there was only a small chance that she would survive. Another stroke would likely come on and take her life.

October 15, 1949, was a warm day for Montana weather. Wilmath had been losing consciousness off and on for the last two days. Lonzo came to the hospital that afternoon to visit. At first he thought that she was asleep. Gradually she opened her eyes and recognized him. She whispered "Bible" to him. He reached over on the table and handed it to her. She grasped it tightly in her hands and clutched it to her body. Then she went back to sleep, with the Bible in that same position, when he left. He tiptoed out of the room, not wanting to disturb her.

It was close to five o'clock when he left the hospital. It was such a nice evening, not quite dark, but still warm for that time of year. He decided to drive up to the old ranch and look around. He headed north of town and turned down the drive along the row of hedge, where he stopped the car. Getting out of the vehicle, he looked around his old home, then out toward the Bridger Mountains. Suddenly, he couldn't believe what he was seeing! Old Baldy was brilliant with light! No, it couldn't be! He looked away, wiping his eyes, and at that exact moment a whiff of lilacs filled the air! Now he knew he must be awfully tired — lilacs didn't bloom that time of year! He looked at the mountain again — the intense glow he had seen radiating from the mountain was not there! So it had been his imagination! Taking his railroad watch out of his pocket, he saw that it was 5:30 p.m. It was getting late and getting dark, too — time to be getting back to town to the house! He got in the car and drove south.

After Lonzo left the hospital at five o'clock, two nurses entered Wilmath's room. She was still sleeping with the Bible held close to her body. The nurses knew it was time to check her pulse and temperature. They stood on each side of her bed. Nurse Mary Parkhurst reached down to take the woman's pulse, while Nurse Betsy Moran began shaking down the thermometer. At that moment Wilmath's eyes opened wide! She was staring straight ahead, seemingly unaware that either nurse was standing beside her. Then her lips started to move, and she spoke in an audible whisper: "Seba, dear, we're together at last!" Then her eyes closed — never to open again. She drew one gasping breath, and it was her last!

"She's gone!" Mary Parkhurst said to Betsy. Betsy looked at her watch — it was 5:30 p.m.

"Did you hear what she said right before she closed her eyes?"

"She said, 'Seba, dear, we're together at last.' "

"That's what I thought she said," Betsy agreed. Mary started to pull the sheet up over the dead woman's face, while Betsy began to remove the Bible from the hands that were holding it. As she slowly removed the book, she noticed that one of the woman's fingers had been marking a certain place between the pages. She opened the Bible up wide at the place, only to see a round hard circle of old dried grass drop out onto the bed.

"What is that thing that just fell out of her Bible?" Mary asked.

"It's just some old dried grass," answered Betsy, with a puzzled look on her face.

Lonzo drove into his driveway at 621 North Rouse. It was totally dark now. He turned the car motor off and got out at the side of the house. He walked up on the porch, and as he was turning the doorknob, the phone was ringing!